PERSONAL INFORMATION MANAGEMENT

PERSONAL INFORMATION MANAGEMENT

TOOLS AND TECHNIQUES FOR ACHIEVING PROFESSIONAL EFFECTIVENESS

BARBARA ETZEL AND PETER THOMAS

NEW YORK UNIVERSITY PRESS
Washington Square, New York

HD
69
T54
E89
1996

First published in the U.S.A. in 1996 by
NEW YORK UNIVERSITY PRESS
Washington Square
New York, N.Y. 10003

Library of Congress Cataloging-in-Publication Data
Etzel, Barbara.
Personal information management : tools and techniques
for achieving professional effectiveness / by Barbara Etzel and
Peter J. Thomas.
p.   cm.
Includes bibliographical references and index.
ISBN 0–8147–2199–0
1. Personal information management.   2. Management information
systems.   3. Executives—Time management.   I. Thomas, Peter J.
II. Title.   III. Title: Tools and techniques for achieving
professional effectiveness,
HD69.T54E89   1996
650.1—dc20   96–18451
                                                        CIP

Printed in Great Britain

Contents

List of figures and tables   viii

Preface   x

Acknowledgements   xiii

1   **From the industrial age to the information age**   **1**
The modern executive   3
Information, technology and new ways of doing business   4
Understanding how to achieve effectiveness   5
Investing time in technology   5
Is productivity increasing or decreasing?   6
Tools for time and information management   7

2   **Personal information management**   **8**
'Personal'   8
'Information'   8
'Management'   10
A new skill: personal information management   10
Personal information management: tools and techniques for achieving
professional effectiveness   14
Some general principles   15
About the rest of this book   16

3   **The eight key information actions**   **18**
What is information?   18
Why do we need information?   19
What do we do with information?   19
Eight key information actions   20
Some other perspectives on information   22

4   **'Information overload' and information management**
're-engineering'   **25**
Information overload   25
Changing (or 're-engineering') your approach to information
management   26
'Information re-engineering goals' and their benefits   27
Related re-engineering techniques: time management, conceptual tools and
thinking   29

5 Understanding information management technology   32
A framework for information management technologies: the 'five
technology potentials'   34

6 Personal information technologies: advantages and disadvantages   37
How to choose personal information products   37
How information is stored and managed   38

7 Computer software and hardware products   43
Spreadsheets   44
Accounting software   46
Billing software   47
Word processing   48
Databases   50
Personal organisers/personal information managers (PIMs)   53
E-mail programs   54
Tracking and storage packages   56
How to choose your software program: summary   57
Computer hardware devices   58
Personal digital assistants (PDAs)   59
CD-Rom   61
Computer back-up systems   62
Scanning devices   63
Telecommunications   64
Why are computers so difficult to use?   66
How to make using a computer easier   69
Other computer issues   70

8 Paper-based information products   72
Categories of paper-based information   72
Operating requirements   73
Administrative requirements   77
Fiscal requirements   78
Legal requirements   78
Historical requirements   78

9 Your personal information management strategy   79
Producing and implementing your own personal information management
strategy   80
Benefits of a PIM strategy   84
Roadblocks to effective personal information management   85
Reasons that prompt the implementation of a PIM strategy   94

10 Beginning to implement your personal information management strategy 95

The macro approach   95
The micro approach   96
Scenario: an architect implementing his personal information management strategy   97

11 Maintaining your personal information management strategy 109

File audit   109   110
Completion   110
Ten-second filing operation   110
Learn to make split-second decisions   111
'I'll do it later'   111
Create your conceptual tools   111
Re-engineer your information management   112
Managing daily information flow   112

12 Computing technology and your personal information management strategy 116

How to manage information in the computer   117
Innovative computer-based personal information management strategies   120
A personal information management strategy not using a computer   122

13 Conclusions 125

Technology and change   125
'Techno trends'   126
Predicting technologies   128
Preventing information build-up   129
Some real problems   131
Summary   132

Appendix 1   Key issues in personal information management   135

Appendix 2   Personal information management products   137

References   147

Index   150

List of figures and tables

■ Figures

3.1   The eight key information actions   21
9.1   The importance of information   23
13.1 Technology life cycles   129
13.2 Problems that affect a successful, productive and organised life and career   133

■ Tables

4.1   The time–management marix   30
5.1   A range of information management technologies   33
5.2   Technologies and the eight key information actions   35
5.3   The five technology potentials   36
7.1   Spreadsheets: information storage or production?   45
7.2   Do you really need a spreadsheet?   45
7.3   Accounting packages: information storage or production?   46
7.4   Accounting packages: do you really need one?   47
7.5   Billing packages: information storage or production?   48
7.6   Do you really need a billing package?   48
7.7   Word processors: information storage or production?   49
7.8   Word processors: do you really need one?   49
7.9   Preformatted databases: information storage or production?   51
7.10 Do you really need a preformatted database?   51
7.11 Non-preformatted databases: information storage or production?   52
7.12 Do you really need a non-preformatted database?   52
7.13 Personal organiser: information storage or production?   53
7.14 Do you really need a personal organiser?   54
7.15 E-mail: information storage or production?   55
7.16 Do you really need an e-mail system?   56
7.17 Tracking and storage packages: information storage or production?   57
7.18 Do you really need a tracking and storage program?   57
7.19 PDAs: information storage or production?   60
7.20 Do you really need a PDA?   60
7.21 CD-Rom: information storage or production?   61

7.22   Do you need a CD-Rom?   62
7.23   Scanners: information storage or production?   64
7.24   Do you really need a scanner?   64
9.1   PIM strategy development chart   80
9.2   PIM strategy benefits questionnaire   86

Preface

No matter how much times change, events tend to repeat themselves. For example, when the telephone was first introduced, it was used and initially promoted as a 'telegraph' – an instantly familiar technology – and users had subsequently to be educated about the concept of 'the telephone' and how it could be used. In 1907, half of the telephones in the USA were owned by companies other than AT&T. That meant consumers had to pay bills to several different phone companies to be able to reach subscribers on a different system (Lubar, 1993, pp.127–31). Another example is the phonograph. The basic phonograph design was constantly being improved by Thomas Edison and his employees in the 1880s and 1890s. A phonograph that sold for $100 in 1896 dropped to $20 in 1897 and to $10 for a stripped-down machine in 1899 (Lubar, 1993, p.172).

Technological advances were also blamed for the ills of society. New methods to set type, cheaper paper production from wood pulp and better presses helped increase the availability and affordability of newspapers and books. Leading thinkers and social critics condemned the changes caused by 'loss of innocence' and the rapid pace of change. George Beard, an American doctor and social critic, listed the telegraph and the newspaper among the five causes of 'nervousness', a pernicious disease he thought characterised Americans at the end of the nineteenth century (Lubar, 1993, p.33).

Now look at the situation today. 'Social ills' and in particular stress are just as prevalent today as they were at the beginning of the twentieth century. Information flooding at us from numerous sources, stress and being too busy are all problems that people complain of today. And, as with the phonograph and the modern printing press, these problems are often blamed on technology. A further parallel is rapid decreases in prices of technology – and even faster increases in power, particularly in the computing industry. By the time you are reading this, the new, top of the line 125mHz Pentium computer with a massive hard disk will probably be easily surpassed by something faster, better and frustratingly less expensive. Finally, many customers are again paying more than one phone bill. They have different bills for their fax, mobile, pager and telephone lines, even though it is all communications technology. And, particularly in the USA, competition for a long distance phone service has led to frequent switching between carriers in order to get the best deal.

So has anything really changed in the last 100 years, or have we just forgotten the lessons and experiences of previous generations? One important distinction exists to explain what is going on today. Technological advances 100 years ago benefited only the wealthy and the literate – a small portion of the population.

Today almost everyone can afford to purchase information and new technology. Even at the rapidly decreasing price of $20, a phonograph was well beyond the financial grasp of most people; today computers costing £1000 are affordable for many people.

We find ourselves again in the midst of a technological and information revolution. The benefits to be gained from the use of technology are enormous but the issues and problems that must be addressed before individual users can take full advantage of these benefits may be daunting. For example, many people can afford, and have already signed up with, services providing connections to 'on-line' information services or to the 'Internet'. However, the gulf between the advantages of the Internet and the reality of not being able to connect (your modem refuses to work, the system won't accept your password, you have the wrong shape telephone plug) or understand its operation (how do I get this to print?) is very wide. Even for those experiencing few technical problems, the issue may become one of what to do with all of the wonderful information you have downloaded – where do you store it?

Even with technological advances, familiar problems still remain. We are still looking for lost paper documents and wondering where we put that file. Instead of eliminating paper in the office, technology can be argued to have had the opposite effect. The amount of paper has increased drastically, with no decrease in sight: in 1992 in the USA businesses generated over *2.5 trillion* pieces of paper (Lubar, 1993, p.37). And more arrives each day, making the term 'information overload' a grim reality.

Seeking answers, many people have looked towards what has come to be known as 'time management'. Time management techniques provide valuable assistance to professionals wanting to pack more into their working day, but many are beginning to find that true personal effectiveness requires more than just 'managing time'. While people have been busy using methods for successfully managing their time, there has been a steady build-up of papers, electronic mail and reading materials that are constantly arriving and demanding attention. And the new tools that promise to make work easier are, mostly, computer-based. Before we can *save* time, we must *spend* time learning how to use the computer. We also must set up a system to manage our paper-based information which, despite the availability of technology, often piles up.

There is little time available to learn these new techniques. Indeed everything must be accomplished quickly. The pressure is increasing for professionals to become more effective, achieve better results faster, and be more flexible and versatile than ever before. The problem that faces many professionals is how to achieve these results – to use information resources effectively and save time. This describes the core issues professionals are dealing with and points towards the skill needed to resolve the situation – what we call in this book *personal information management*. We would like to convince you that what the phrase 'time management' signified for the 1980s, 'personal information management' signifies for the 1990s and beyond.

The issues of 'information overload', the links between new and old technologies, the hidden problems of new technologies and new ways of managing information are the things we talk about in this book, and the things we will help you understand and deal with effectively.

BARBARA ETZEL
PETER THOMAS

▌Acknowledgements

We would like express our eternal gratitude to Helen Pitter, who, with more good humour and efficiency than it seems reasonable to expect of anyone, offered us invaluable help in completing this book. Over several months she read the entire manuscript several times and handled numerous telephone calls, meetings, e-mail messages and faxes – all of which made the process of a transatlantic writing project almost painless. We know that there is little we could teach her about effective personal information management.

All errors and omissions which remain are of course our responsibility.

B.E.
P.T.

CHAPTER 1

From the industrial age to the information age

At the turn of the century we were still living in rural areas. We might have heard about the first plane flight (in 1903) and our most complex office machine was the manual typewriter. In our offices were 'information management tools' such as a Rolodex, and ledgers to keep track of numerical information. Mail delivery was slow, and electronic mail (*e-mail*) voice mail and overnight mail did not exist. In 1893 the vertical filing cabinet was introduced, replacing copy books, flat files and letter boxes which stored information in the order it was received. Towards the middle of the twentieth century office equipment and procedures became more sophisticated. The first successful electric typewriter was introduced in 1935 by IBM (Lupton, 1993, pp.45–7). The telephone, while it changed in design and many more people began using it, essentially was unchanged in its functionality.

Offices in the early part of the twentieth century were following a 'production-line' model of work. Large companies employed hundreds of employees, usually women, as typists. They took the information that was presented to them and typed it into the machine and produced a letter, report or memo. The typist did the 'production' part; her boss used the information and acted upon it. Early versions of the typewriter, adding machine or telephone were strictly 'production tools' – they were not able to hold information. Another dimension has been added to the equation. In addition to the production function, each piece of office equipment now *stores* information. Our phones store the numbers of frequently called people, and our messages can be retrieved and stored in voice mail systems. Instead of only producing letters or other documents, computers and electronic typewriters store information.

While this can save a great deal of time, and provide more benefits, it can also produce complications. Now the modern employee has to understand, amongst other things:

- how to store and retrieve information from computers, phones, and e-mail systems;
- how to use numerous application programs for computers;
- how to solve problems connected with the use of each machine.

Employees today have more power at their fingertips than ever before, but the complexity that they must deal with has increased tremendously. The speed with which information can be obtained also decreases the expected response time: instead of putting a reply in the mail within a few days, people expect an *immediate* answer to their e-mail, fax or overnight letter. And while voice mail is an excellent tool for one-way conversations or detailed messages, it becomes a nightmare if the person you are calling is avoiding you, or you must speak with a live person. Previous generations only had to deal with primarily cosmetic changes of the design of office equipment. Is it any wonder that business professionals are experiencing trouble coping?

Beginning in the 1970s, and more forcefully in the 1980s, professionals were encouraged to add time management to their repertoire of tools. This was happening just as people were beginning to experience 'information overload'. Now you have the typical business professional struggling to (1) learn to use a personal computer, and incorporate this into his daily routine; (2) cope with an increasing volume of information, both electronic and paper-based; and (3) manage increasing loads of work while using time management techniques to work more effectively.

As one might imagine, this scenario helps produce 'stressed-out' professionals. According to surveys by Dianna Booher, the average white-collar worker receives 145 pages of printed material per week. Most people can not keep up, and as a result most paperwork gets skimmed and never read (Booher, 1986, p.105). Amongst the plethora of statistics in the popular press about 'information overload' there are many that are interesting. For instance, according to an article published in 1994 by the Association of Management, Americans consume paper at twice the rate of the British and the Japanese; another headline-grabbing statistic states that the documentation for a Boeing 747 weighs more than the plane itself (Association of Management, 1994, p.24).

We have all come to understand the value of information, and information management, to business in the 1990s. The rate of change in the way businesses operate in the last 20 years is largely a result of the 'information revolution', in which businesses are using information and technology to become more flexible and responsive to their customers' needs. Information is also being used to accomplish more work with fewer employees. All organisations, to survive, need to manage information and use computers as 'information management systems' – from the simple databases we see in the smallest business to the large and complex decision-aiding 'executive information systems' used by large corporations. These systems have had an enormous impact on the working lives of every professional, changing the ways in which the organisation operates.

But perhaps the most enormous change is at the 'personal', rather than organisational level. Every day we all must deal with more and more information, delivered through an increasing number of media, which requires learning time and more effective management to achieve the best results for our personal performance. And often these media are ones that we do not inherently understand, or know how to use. Nowhere is this change more noticeable than in the data-processing department. Computers were once the domain of 'computer professionals' working behind locked doors. Now that computing power has increased exponentially, and the size of the boxes it fits in has reduced, computing power has arrived on each employee's desktop. Filing responsibilities also have shifted dramatically. Filing, and managing information, used to be the sole responsibility of a secretary or large records departments. As companies have 'downsized' and turned more information over to individual employees to manage, each employee has had to take more responsibility for managing his own information.

Corporations have known for some time how crucial it is to have a 'corporate information plan' that details the resources and the type of information that are important. Now it is necessary is for individuals to develop their own 'personal' information plan that outlines what information is important and how it will be stored and retrieved. One of the important messages of this book is that information management can be seen from a 'personal' perspective – not the large scale organisation effects of the 'information revolution', but the effect on individual professionals. We will suggest that to achieve personal effectiveness requires a new way of looking at managing information from this personal perspective. We can illustrate this, and some of the problems we will be trying to tackle, in the following scenario.

■ The Modern Executive

Picture the modern executive at 8:30 am.

He grabs his bulging briefcase as he heads out of the door, quickly picks up the newspaper off the lawn, and shoves it into his over-filled briefcase. He drives to work, parks his car, walks inside and greets his secretary, who hands him a six-inch stack of mail. He walks to his desk then lays the mail on top of the Wilson *project papers. That pile spills onto the departmental budget papers.* Another crisis around the bend, *he thinks sarcastically.* Better get to it today.

Now he is feeling overwhelmed. He drops his brief case behind the desk. Instead of hitting the floor it lands on the Miller *papers.* These need to go to storage, *he thinks. It will be another six months before Sam Miller is ready to begin the project, if he ever is. But first he wants to sort through the file and weed out the unnecessary papers and put everything in order. He could have his secretary do it, but he wants to make sure nothing is incorrectly thrown out. He pulls out the newspaper from his briefcase and spends four minutes looking at the headlines.* Time to get to work, *he thinks, and tosses the paper to the far left corner of his desk onto his reading pile, where two week-old newspapers, four lengthy reports and a month's worth of magazines sit. It's only 9:15 Monday morning, and already he's exhausted and overwhelmed.* Another day, another dollar, *and another 100 pounds of paper to sift through and manage.*

He decides he needs to call John, a client, and begins to think where his number is. He turns on the computer, and pulls up his database. He doesn't really like using the computer, but concedes it has some advantages. He finds the number; however it is John's old number. He moved offices three weeks ago. He knows he wrote the number down somewhere. He looks in his Rolodex, but it's not there. He goes to the file cabinet for John's file. He is looking for the change of address card that John mailed. He pages through the file and after a minute finds it and makes his call. Once he is finished with the call, he considers changing the data in the computer, but discards that idea. It would take too much time and, besides, he's not sure how to work the database program that well. He'll just remember the address card next time he needs to change it.

The person described above is not in a unique situation, nor is he 'incompetent' or 'inferior'. He is struggling in a business environment that has increased in complexity with the introduction of computers and other new technology. Instead of knowing that all his information is on paper, the possibility exists that it *may* be on the computer. And, while the computer brings many advantages, it also brings a completely new way of storing and recalling information that is different to that used in the past. It also requires the adoption of new habits.

Several other factors are also affecting his performance. Twenty years ago the work assigned to him would have been shared by several other people. It is not surprising, then, that he continually feels behind. He is wondering if he is next in line to be made redundant. He is also expected to keep up with new developments and information that arrive every day in the form of letters, memos, e-mail and trade journals, not to mention a new software program (or two).

■ Information, technology and new ways of doing business

What our busy professional is experiencing is the pressures generated by the convergence of several forces: *information, technology, new business processes* and *new personal goals*. The situation is complex:

- in order to achieve his goals, the professional must keep up with new developments, and this largely means sifting through the mass of paper-based and digital information available;
- to build and maintain networks of colleagues, the professional must increasingly use computer-based communication media – such as the Internet – as an essential part of keeping in touch;
- new business processes also mean an increase in 'computer-mediated' work, using for example e-mail, corporate databases or executive information systems.

Understanding how to achieve effectiveness is not easy. Many professionals only have the time to update themselves when absolutely necessary. And even then, updating to new technologies – understanding and using them – is often ad hoc.

▌Understanding how to achieve effectiveness

The situation we have briefly described in our scenario points out a new concept and a new set of skills that professionals are having to grasp: *personal information management*. The skills it describes are well known and recognised as valuable. For example, how many times have we searched for a letter that we know we saw a few days ago and now cannot find? Or perhaps you intended to call a friend on Saturday afternoon. Her phone number is on your computer database at the office, so you wrote it on a Post-it note on Friday afternoon and put it in your wallet. However you cannot find the Post-it note now. You decide to use your notebook computer to dial into the computer at work. After trying for 15 minutes to connect, you decide you are doing something wrong or the program is not working properly. *So much for modern technology*, you think.

While few people would argue about the benefits technology has brought, it must be realised that technology has also increased the complexity of offices and managing personal information. Part of the reason for the complexity is that people must learn a complete set of new skills to use the technology successfully. Until these are firmly grasped, using a computer or another technological device will seem confusing and awkward. While many people complained about the complexity of new entertainment technology, such as a VCR, the reality was that, after a few tries or a few hours, the machine was mastered. If that did not work an appeal to the 12-year-old in the family quickly took care of the problem. Offices are increasingly complex places to work, compared to even a decade ago. This complexity in turn causes problems for people and eats into productivity gains that otherwise might have been achieved from the use of technology.

Even the experts are occasionally stumped. In his book, *Being Digital*, Nicholas Negroponte, Professor of Media Technology at MIT, asked the question, 'Why do computers (and bank statements) have to be so needlessly complicated?' (Negroponte, 1995, p.89). Negroponte is not a computer novice. He has used computers for many years, and spends a minimum of three hours a day in front of his computer. If experience and practice can not prevent an experienced computer user from declaring that computers are complicated and frustrating, what can?

Computers, many times unjustly, are also endlessly blamed for the problems users experience. The 1978 *Old Farmers' Almanac* offered this assessment of computers: 'To err is human but to really foul things up requires a computer.'

▌Investing time in technology

Technology is just one of the factors that is creating difficulty. *Time* is another. In an effort to keep up with new developments, many people have great intentions to read magazines and trade journals. However their reading pile is now 10 inches high and two more magazines have just arrived in the mail. The question then becomes one of how to create the time to read the information. There are other questions too. Where should you store it once you have read it? How are you going to remember you have it? Do you file it somewhere so you can retrieve it later? Once these questions have been answered, a trade magazine sends you a database of industry participants on a CD-Rom. *This is a wonderful idea*, you think; however you do not actually *have* a CD-Rom; you consider getting one (for a few minutes) and wonder how beneficial it will be; you do not want to fall behind, but you already have too much to do, and one more project (to research the best-buy CD-Rom and then learn how to use it) is not what you want; nor do you have the time for this project.

The true value of a product must take into consideration the time it takes to research and purchase it, as well as the time it will take to learn it. And, once that product is learned, be certain that *even more time* must be expended on problem-solving exercises when it does not do what you think it should.

■ Electronic mail

To take another example, electronic mail (e-mail) is another area where both time and complexity have increased. The idea of e-mail is wonderful. It provides almost instantaneous communication without the user having to play 'phone tag'. Also one message can be routed to many people. But what do you do with this information after it is received? Can it be deleted once it is read? Can it be saved in an e-mail 'in-basket' or should it be printed and put in a paper file? What happens if your software is not working correctly? You never had to figure out how to 'retrieve' a paper letter. These situations add complexity to the task of managing information.

Time is also an issue with e-mail. You have noticed that you are taking about 20 minutes to read and answer your electronic mail. This might be okay if your internal mail and postal mail had decreased in the meantime. However beware: a *Wall Street Journal* article in 1991 cited the example of a software engineer who returned from a three-week assignment and faced his e-mail. Awaiting him were 1000 messages. Now that is information overload. (Hirsch, 1991, p.B1)

■ Is productivity increasing or decreasing?

Technology has produced more ways than ever before to help us save time and manage our information more efficiently, but is it really producing any noticeable benefits? If you can not state the benefits, and you still have many instances where you can not find what you need when you need it, you are not alone. In fact, many people have cited statistics showing that, in the last two decades, blue-collar productivity has increased 90 per cent, while white-collar productivity has increased only 4 per cent.

However this calculation was made in the early 1970s (by Alan Purchase of SRI International) and focused on the productivity increase between the early 1960s and 1970s. His research was published in a number of private client studies and was picked up widely. This calculation was erroneously attributed to the United States Labor Department's Bureau of Labor Statistics (as stated in Panko, 1985). It is not reliable to estimate overall national office productivity trends: instead of looking at the entire economy, you can only determine productivity trends in a single segment of it. Panko's figures show that, for private businesses, productivity grew at a compounded annual productivity growth rate of 1.4 per cent. Manufacturing productivity grew at 2.7 per cent during this period and the productivity for the office-intensive sectors of the United States federal government grew at a rate of 1.7 per cent. Looking at a smaller time period, between 1977 and 1981, the productivity growth rate for private business was 0.1 per cent, for manufacturing was 1.1 per cent and for office-intensive sectors of the United States federal government was 3.0 per cent.

Statistics in the areas of white-collar or office productivity often make for interesting reading and shocking headlines, however, they must be evaluated carefully before we make judgements.

■ Tools for time and information management

Whatever the cause of our struggle to manage our personal information, one thing is certain. While individual people are affected, the cause of the problem does not necessarily begin with individual inadequacies. Rather this a new problem that affects all of us. We have so many different software programs, filing systems and time management systems, as well as our old technologies such as paper files, that it is very difficult to pick the ones that will help us. Two extremes of the same problem can occur: one is that we adapt so many tools that we trip over what we are doing by trying to remember where different information is stored; the other is that, out of frustration and a lack of understanding of how to use these tools, we immediately dismiss any potential benefit of new technologies and continue in our current ways, which may not be the most efficient solution.

There is an abundance of different productivity and personal information management tools. They are supposed to help us increase our productivity and make life easier, but in reality they often do not.

CHAPTER 2

Personal information management

We have looked at parallels between 'old' technology and 'old ways' of managing information and the situation facing us today. We have also suggested that professionals in a changing business environment need a new set of skills to achieve effectiveness. In our view, *personal information management* will give us the ability to cope with this changing environment. What exactly *is* 'personal information management'?

■ 'Personal'

Personal refers to information that is particular to an individual and is necessary to the performance of his or her job. While a corporation will have a wide variety of information, a sales person for that company probably will not be too concerned about the money spent on salaries for the production department. However that information is very important to the vice-president of production, as well as to the accounting department. What the sales person will be very concerned about are the names of his contacts at client companies, the contact person, the address, the phone number and the account history. This information is of little use to the accounting department. The information clearly is the *property* of the corporation, but it is *personal* to that sales person because it must be used by him and be easily accessed.

■ 'Information'

Information is another term that it is useful to define as it is not as simple as it appears. Thirty years ago, information existed in fewer forms than today. E-mail, which for practical purposes did not exist ten years ago (other than in government and academic sources on the Internet) is now just as common as letters and memos. Also there are many computer databases as well as software programs containing important information. Information arrives in various forms such as facsimile and voice mail. Information is everything we deal with which in some way informs us about events, problems, actions and people. It may arrive in the form of news heard on the radio, casual gossip about a colleague, or the problems of a corporate project.

Along with information created by new technologies, information still exists in traditional forms such as printed letters and memos; the volume of information has increased in direct proportion with the proliferation of high-speed copiers and personal computers on people's desks; the amount of direct mail and catalogues has increased dramatically. While some of these items can go quickly into the waste-paper basket, others pique the interest of the reader and remain around.

The following are some of those forms of information that we will discuss later in this book.

Electronic computer software programs
    Spreadsheets
    Accounting
    Billing
    Word processors
    Databases
    Personal organisers/calendars
    E-mail programs
    Tracking and storage
Computer hardware devices
    Personal digital assistants
    CD-Roms
    Computer tape back-up
    Scanners
Computer networks that provide access to sundry sources of information
    Internet
    CompuServe
    America On-Line
    Prodigy
    Delphi
Telecommunications
    Pagers
    Voice mail
    Cellphones
    Sophisticated office phones
    Fax
Paper
    Files
    Magazines
    Books
    Newspapers
    Business cards
    Post-it notes
    Wall calendars
    Personal organisers

■ 'Management'

The above list illustrates the variety of information and the tools that transmit and hold it. The *management* aspect of 'personal information management' refers to developing a coherent *strategy* to handle the tools and the information they provide. In order to survive, the modern professional must have a coherent plan to control and manage the information that is presenting itself for attention.

If there is no management, and if the information just lies where it was last placed, the result will be chaos and an ever-increasing number of items which appear on every day's 'to-do list' and inevitably get pushed onto the 'I'll do it one day' list. Usually, however, 'one day' never arrives. The management in 'personal information management' can take many forms. Basically, if we decide to throw all 'junk' mail out, that is one management technique. As drastic as that may sound, that can be one valid strategy for dealing with too much information. The key to using this strategy successfully is developing a clear idea of what information is needed and what is not.

'Management' also refers to *where* we store information. Is it going to stay in the PC, in a clearly defined directory where it can be retrieved within a matter of seconds? Is it going to be printed out and put in a paper file in the filing cabinet? If so, will it also stay on the computer? What about e-mail received from colleagues on the computer network. What should be done with the information? By increasing the variables of creating and sending information, the complexity of managing information also increases.

Technology has provided additional benefits to help manage information, but it has also brought with it increased complexity and additional challenges. Once upon a time, managing information required no more effort than putting a piece of paper in the filing cabinet and putting a name and phone number in a Rolodex. Those days of simplicity are gone.

■ A new skill: personal information management

We have provided a basic definition of personal information management – one which we will develop throughout the book, looking at specific ways in which it is an essential concept for today's professional. The practical dimension of personal information management is that it suggests a new set of skills, and some new ways of managing information. Before taking a look at these new ways of managing information, it is interesting to explore how the closely related concepts of 'information management' and 'time management' evolved.

■ Calendars, diaries and Filofaxes

In the early development of many cultures little information existed in written form. Instead information was passed in conversations. The earliest efforts at providing a structure for people to group their time or experiences were calendars. The first efforts to develop a calendar extend as far back as 2000 BC, when stone alignments were used, possibly to determine the length of the solar year by marking the sun's progress across the horizon. One of the biggest holidays today is New Year's Day, which is a time for parties as well as declarations of new beginnings. It is interesting to note that this date was chosen for what is now a non-event. In 153 BC, Roman consuls began taking office on 1 January, which became the first day of the year. This date was continued as the beginning of the year in the Julian and Gregorian calendar (Grolier Electronic Publishing, 1995).

Today we have taken the calendar to the next step, that of a diary, and then have taken one step further and created *Filofaxes* and other more sophisticated time management systems. In 1921 a British Army officer posted in the USA, Colonel Disney, came up with the idea of an 'organiser', a folder with leaves that contained information useful to technical users, engineers and scientists. The idea was a useful one and adaptable, so Colonel Disney thought it might succeed in Britain. He had friends who ran a printing company and a manufacturing business with a retail operation linked to stationery products. He obtained manufacturing and distribution rights in the UK and incorporated his business, calling it *Norman and Hill Ltd*. The success of the product was spurred on by the company's first employee, a temporary secretary by the name of Grace Scurr. It was Grace who coined the word 'Filofax' in 1925. Growth in sales of the Filofax was modest until the Second World War, perhaps because people's lives were much more leisurely. The product began to catch on with doctors who made house calls and found the product very useful for jotting down details about patients. Journalists also discovered the value of a system for the person whose life was a continual set of appointments, meetings, notes and facts.

As is often the case, war causes terrible damage, but can also create opportunity, which it did for Filofax. On 30 December 1940 Grace Scurr arrived at work, after a night of bombing, and found that her office did not exist any more. The air-raid warden told her that her office was gone, she had lost everything and that was the end of her business. Grace opened her handbag and said, 'Oh no, it's not. It's all in here. Good-bye.' Grace had kept her own Filofax, which contained all of her customer records. She had updated her Filofax each day and took it home each night. Even though her office was destroyed, the records survived. Out of the ashes of war, the Filofax grew in usage as well in the variety of information it stored (Sinclair, 1988, pp.1–5).

■ The 'paperless office'

Before the Filofax was developed other people were beginning to notice there was a problem in dealing with information and the paper it was held on. The 'Paper Explosion' was first noted in 1908 when US President Theodore Roosevelt issued *Executive Order No. 937*, which attempted to combat paperwork. It created the Interdepartmental Statistical Committee, whose purpose was to suggest ways to eliminate unnecessary duplication of work (Ridge, 1969, p.15). In 1934 the *National Archives* were created. They began a two-year survey which revealed chaotic record-keeping methods in government agencies, with duplication of records and non-uniform standards prevailing (Maedke *et al.*, 1981, p.19).

Soon after, private enterprise began to experience the paper explosion and its financial impact. For example, Marks & Spencer decided to eliminate excess forms and paperwork: in the late 1950s the company got rid of 26 million forms and reduced its staff from 27 000 to 20 000. The result was that the company saved money on paperwork and staff salaries and sales doubled between 1963 and 1972. To do this, Marks & Spencer's top management 'wandered around' the offices looking for unnecessary paperwork. This was an effective weapon against paperwork. If top management said a form was unnecessary, no one argued and the form was quickly destroyed (Rayner, 1975, pp.8–14). The US government was also taking another look at efficiency and paperwork levels. In 1947–9 a commission headed by former President Herbert Hoover made recommendations on improvements in the record-keeping function. A second study in 1955 drew further attention to the mounting paperwork problem, and placed responsibility for its control at the high management rather than the clerical level (Place and Pophum, 1966, p.9).

Today the issue is not efficiency for its own sake but rather the reduction of unnecessary expense that can be calculated and traced back to the bottom line. According to one research study, it costs the typical company $7000 in materials and paperwork to create, handle and file all of the contents of an ordinary four-drawer file cabinet over the life of the cabinet (Maedke *et al.*, 1981); annual storage costs of information in each active four-drawer filing cabinet with about 18 000 pages is cited at $2160 according to the National Business Forms Association (the costs include the salaries of file clerks, so, if you are a manager, adjust the estimate accordingly). Out of those documents, 85 per cent are never referred to again and 45 per cent are duplicate copies (Booher, 1986, p.104).

Yet again in the 1980s, the US federal government got into the act of tackling paperwork. In 1980 the Paperwork Reduction Act was passed. On 25 October 1982 President Reagan signed legislation calling for a White House Conference on Productivity. In May 1995 President Bill Clinton renewed the Paperwork Reduction Act: The National Federation of Independent Business estimates it will reduce small firms' governmental paperwork demands by 10 per cent (*Industry Week*, 1995, p.71). In Britain, the government in July 1995 announced a new war on waste and a major drive to cut paperwork and streamline administration (Brown, 1995, p.1).

And, if further evidence were necessary, Dianna Booher, in a 1986 study, cites research conducted by form designers and record management experts which reveals the following statistics:

- 60 per cent of all clerical work is checking, filing, and retrieving information. Only 40 per cent of clerical time is spent on more important tasks such as data processing and communication.
- 75 per cent of documents that are retained are never referred to again.

- 3 per cent of filed documents needed again have been misfiled.
- For every dollar spent on printing forms, $20–$80 is spent on processing, copying, distribution, storage and destruction.

A survey by the Dartnell Institute, as cited in a productivity brief by the American Productivity Center, showed the following results:

- 70 per cent more records are retained than are needed;
- 45 per cent of filing space is used to store duplicates and records of doubtful reference value;
- 95 per cent of all references to records are made to documents less than three years old. (Heijn, 1982, p.5)

How did this happen? How did we get embroiled in this mountain of papers? Booher offers an explanation based on heredity. She says we are born with the idea that important agreements and events are recorded on paper – births, deaths, grades, taxes, wills, marriages, social security numbers or insurance policies. School reinforces the importance of recording information on paper: extra paperwork on school projects produces a higher grade; assignments for papers are made according to length, not according to the objective; students are told to write a five-page paper, rather than being told to write a paper that is clear and proves their point. In addition to heredity, Booher also suggests that personality disorders play a significant part in explaining why we have too many papers in the workplace today. Reasons include:

- paranoia about being blamed for errors;
- distrust of anyone who does not 'put it in writing';
- inability to delegate without constant 'report backs';
- phobias about computers and information not in hard copy;
- lack of confidence in being articulate in a face-to-face conversation.

■ The 'time management' concept

As the 1980s approached, 'time management' became a key concept. The point was not just keeping track of details and information any more, it was to *manage time*, as everyone was increasingly busy. Time management concepts were presented in seminars (usually lasting several hours) accompanied by 'time management book' that was intended to organise your schedule along with your projects and 'to-do' lists. In the late 1980s the same companies began designing software programs to use in place of the paper-based books.

On a smaller scale, the stationery products used to schedule appointments and maintain addresses have increased in complexity. They may now contain, in addition to the calendar, a place for names and addresses as well as sheets listing to-dos and projects. It is not a simple matter to buy a calendar any more (as anyone who has walked into an office supply store will understand). You have to hunt through *hundreds* of different books to find the one you need. Everything from the basic calendar to 'organisers' that come in different shapes and sizes and have many useful inserts and 'add-ons' can be found.

Yet people are still searching for assistance. A new profession – that of a *professional organiser* – has been created. This profession started in the USA on the east and west coasts in the early 1980s. In 1985 the National Association of Professional Organizers was formally established by a group of organisers in Los Angeles who had met informally for two years as a networking and support group. The goals of the association are to promote the profession of organising, educate the public about the field of organising and provide support, education and a networking forum for the membership. As a companion to time management, many seminars were developed on 'setting goals' and 'managing results'. They all focused on how to do a better job, achieve better results and make work easier.

While we firmly believe in the value of time management, we also believe that 'managing time' is not the major problem facing professionals today. It is to the explosion of information and the new ways in which information arrives, *in addition to* the problem of managing time, that we should look to achieve professional effectiveness. Of course, social trends such as an increasing number of women in paid employment in addition to handling their domestic activities have made the problem more pressing. There is simply much more do, and more information to deal with.

Regardless of whether you are a busy corporate executive or a homemaker, you will be attempting to cope with 'information overload'. The trouble is not *getting* information, it is sorting through and organising the information that does exist.

Personal information management: tools and techniques for achieving professional effectiveness

There is a way out of the situation we have described. With careful thought and creation of a strategy, the problems of information overload can be managed with what we will call in this book a 'personal information management strategy' or a 'PIM strategy'. Recognising your *need* for such a strategy is the first step. The next is to be informed about the many 'personal information products' that exist, and to develop knowledge and skills to allow you to decide what tools will help you most. Then you will need to develop and implement a PIM Strategy: practical ways in which you can deal with, amongst other things, the information explosion and the overload it has created. And of course, the final step is to ensure that your PIM strategy is effective and remains so. This means, amongst other things, looking for opportunities to 'add value' to information and making yourself aware of new technologies which will affect how you manage information.

■ Some general principles

In addition to the details that will be discussed further in this book, some general principles will help you to start thinking about a PIM strategy and its usefulness.

■ Define what information is important

Today there is more information than ever before. It is often inexpensive to *receive* information, whether it is in a publication or a computer on-line service, but the time is never available to allow all of this information to be read. There is so much information that the day could easily be spent reading on-line news and information as well as perusing magazines.

■ Be cautious about what you save

While we often like to save information for future use, we need to be cautious about what we save. The statistics we have looked at previously show that we save much more than we ever refer to again. And even if you want to read something in more detail later it is likely you will never have any extra time to spend looking at non-urgent items.

■ Have a system for what you save and where you put it

Much has been written about the benefits of having a good filing system, but you must also have a plan for where you store e-mail, computer files or phone numbers. Having a computer, or 'hand-held personal information manager' only compounds the problem if you have not thought out and developed your strategy.

■ Use your brain more effectively

When all else fails, *use your brain*. Although this seems a trite comment, studies show that we only actively use less than 1 per cent of our brain power. And we do not give ourselves enough credit for our ability to remember the information we need when we need it (Buzan, 1984, p.13).

■ Manage information technology

The previous principles apply to any kind of 'technology' (including paper), but there are some other issues which relate specifically to information technology:

How do I incorporate important e-mail information into my word processing software or integrate it into my paper files? Should I just store it in my e-mail program?

I enter my client information three different times: into my Rolodex, my word-processing software and my billing software. Isn't that a waste of time? I thought computers were supposed to save time, not create more work. And sometimes I will find an incorrect address in one of them, months after that person has moved.

I have all my documents and letters saved on the computer, and I also have a copy in the file. Isn't this redundant?

I keep a to-do list on my computer in a personal information manager software program. I make notes to myself throughout the day on Post-it notes and the phone calls that I need to return are saved in my voice mail. Now all I have to do is remember where everything is.

Before any technology is implemented, a well-thought out strategy must be established. This must include a realistic look at the *cost* of the technology, compared to the expected *benefits*. It also must include the *learning time* required to use the new technology effectively. Also the implementation time and cost must be considered. If the benefits are not great enough, or if the cost is too high, then, even though the technology is good, it may not be appropriate in this situation.

In addition to technology issues, any PIM strategy must take into consideration individual concerns. First, the most important awareness is that there is no single 'prescription' for everyone. Each bit of technology or usage of information must be closely matched to the individual's needs, understanding and liking. If it is not then, no matter how 'useful' or popular the product is, it is inappropriate. In adapting technology, the person must assess how they best retain and recall information. If people are visually oriented and recall information by seeing where it is, putting that information into a computer (especially non-Windows programs) or putting it into a filing cabinet may be equally unworkable solutions. If words are used to recall where information is, a Windows-based program that is heavy on pictures and graphics may be annoying.

And, while this is a less-tangible issue, psychological factors must be examined. Why are some people 'extreme packrats' who insist on saving everything, even though it is apparent to everyone else that they can not possibly find anything, other than what might be on the top layer?

■ About the rest of this book

Our intention throughout this book is to provide you with a system for analysing your information and then showing you how you can construct your own PIM strategy based upon your individual situation. We will give you ideas to think about and situations to help you determine your strategy, alongside some specific actions you can take. However we have purposely avoided producing a book filled with the 'organisation tips' commonly found in many 'getting yourself organised' types of books. This is because we believe that personal information management is much more complex and dynamic than simply 'getting yourself organised'. Instead we present you with ideas and concepts to consider and implement as your personal situation requires. It is also because, in recognising the need for personal information management as a new concept, we have seen the complexity of the problem: in reading the research literature in areas such as information management, communications, the design of usable computers, time-management and psychology, we have come to appreciate the complex relationships between new technologies and their effects, the psychology of information management and the practical demands placed on professionals today.

The following chapters deal with a range of issues in personal information management and developing a PIM strategy, which include:

- understanding personal information management;
- understanding information and what we do with it;
- understanding different approaches to managing information;
- the tools and technologies are available to help manage information, and their advantages and disadvantages;
- developing a PIM strategy;
- maintaining a PIM strategy;
- new developments which will affect the ways that all of us deal with information.

CHAPTER 3

The eight key information actions

In this chapter we will introduce some of the concepts behind personal information management in detail. First, we will look at the idea of 'information' itself and ask what appear to be some obvious questions about information. The answers to these will be useful in understanding information and how we use it. The point of these questions is to make you aware of 'information' and 'managing information' as important issues. We will then show you a simple framework for understanding information: the *eight key information actions*.

■ What is information?

The first obvious question is 'what is information?' Basically information is anything we deal with which informs us about events, issues, problems, actions and people. Put this way, information might appear to be *everything*, from the e-mail message that arrives on your computer system to the casual gossip about a colleague, or about the problems of a particular project, in the office corridor, to the latest local or international news item.

Although we might regard office gossip as vital professional information – and of course it can be crucial in the work of a professional manager (so much so that MBWA, management by walking around, is a recognised approach where listening to gossip is encouraged) – we view information as the more tangible kind that professionals use in their working lives.

Information comes in various forms and is manipulated using various technologies. This includes information which is stored in paper form (in filing cabinets, notebooks, paper files) and information which is stored, retrieved and communicated through various information technologies (telephone, facsimile, personal computer, e-mail or voice mail). Information is essential if we are to perform effectively as a professional in any occupation – from senior manager to salesperson – and it is the failure to recognise that information can be managed which leads to professional ineffectiveness. New forms of information technology, specifically computer-based technologies, require lots of effort.

■ Why do we need information?

The second obvious question is 'why do we need information?' Information is an essential part of the way we act in the world around us. All of the time we are collecting, taking in, creating and changing information: the daily paper we read at the breakfast table, the radio station we listen to when driving to work, and the mass of communications and documents most professionals process in the course of a day, are all information we deal with.

For the professional, information enables decisions to be made. In business this has been seen as so fundamental that an entire school of management has been developed to ensure that the information we have available is the most appropriate to allow us to make crucial decisions which affect our work. The so-called 'decision-making' school of management (created by Herbert Simon and Peter Drucker) led to the use of 'information management systems' – computer systems which supply information about the work of an organisation. Many professionals are aware of the operation of their organisation's information systems and have strong views on how they can support their work. However this focus on 'corporate-level' information management has not been matched by a focus on the 'individual' and 'personal' side of managing information we discussed in the previous chapter.

In the same way that we use 'corporate databases' to gather information about company performance, many professionals are surrounded by technology which they use to manage their personal information. Where an 'executive information system' (EIS) is used to support decision making about strategy or about planning company-wide, simpler technologies are used every day by professionals to manage their information in order to make decisions.

■ What do we do with information?

The third and final obvious question we will ask is 'what do we do with information?' Consider the following simple scenario, thinking about information and the technologies that are being used.

Robert, a member of a research team, has been invited to give a presentation at an international conference. He submitted the text for the presentation at the conference some months ago in response to an e-mail message calling for scientific contributions in his research field. The text was submitted, as is usual for such conferences, in both paper and electronic form – the latter taking the form of a computer diskette. Robert has kept copies of the electronic submission on his PC and copies of the paper version (which is accompanied by photocopies of the conference registration form, housing form and requirements for audio-visual equipment form) in a project file labelled 'conferences 1995'. In the file are also paper copies of the e-mail messages sent from the conference organising committee which reviewed and accepted the paper and suggested minor changes. Robert has thrown away other correspondence since the paper was submitted. Robert's boss John, the head of the research team, knows that Robert will be attending the conference as he originally forwarded the e-mail message about the conference to Robert and suggested that they write a paper together; if it was accepted, Robert should make the presentation.

The text of the paper, after numerous discussions in team meetings and using e-mail, was written by Robert from sections of text and notes belonging to both of them. Robert finished and proof-read the final draft before sending it to the conference chairman. He sent an e-mail copy of the completed paper to John and another copy, along with the conference details, to the research group's administrator for inclusion in a database showing the research group's submissions for conferences this year.

Now Robert has to organise his trip to the conference. He sends a fax of the dates of the trip to the company which deals with the group's flight bookings and asks them to book the flight which matches the dates he has specified. To make sure they get the exact details, he has faxed rather than telephoned, as it often takes longer to communicate the details to the travel agent by telephone, and by using a fax he can be sure all the details are correct. He also looks at his diary to figure out whether he can stay an extra day to relax and meet some colleagues from another research group. While he is telephoning John to confirm that he will be making the trip, the travel company calls back and leaves a message on Robert's voice mail suggesting several alternative flight arrangements and prices, and several alternative departure times. Robert calls back to discuss the options and confirms the flight he wants. He sends an e-mail message with these details to the research group's administrator so that she can complete the appropriate paperwork to book the flight and tie up the arrangements with the travel company.

■ Eight key information actions

In the above scenario, which is part of everyday life for many professionals, we can see several answers to the question 'what do we do with information?'

1. We *create* information: Robert's conference paper, worked on with John, was created from conversations, notes, records of meetings and new text written by Robert.
2. We *change* information: the paper copies of e-mail messages represent a change in the form of the information (electronic to paper) and the change in the information contained in the text of the presentation (minor amendments to the text following the reviewers' suggestions).
3. We *store* information: the storage of the text of the presentation onto the diskette, a paper printout and in the conferences project file are all forms of storage.
4. We *retrieve* information: Robert retrieves information from his diary to send the fax to the travel company, and retrieves information from his voice mail about the details of the flight.
5. We *integrate* information: Robert integrates the information contained in several sources – the e-mail messages, his personal computer, the call from the travel company, notes in his notebooks about the presentation – and combines it to send off the final presentation text and make arrangements for it to be presented.

6. We also can *make decisions* using information: the information from Robert's diary, the conference organisers and the travel company is used to make a decision about his travel arrangements.
7. We *communicate* information: the fax to the travel company, and the e-mail messages about the travel arrangements all rely on the communication of information.
8. And finally we *discard* information: Robert discards the information in previous correspondence as not useful.

It is easy to forget in our everyday use of information that we do all of these things: create, change, store, retrieve, integrate, make decisions, communicate and discard. They are activities which are essential to most professionals. These eight key information actions are important because they help us to think about the possibilities that we have when working with information.

In Figure 3.1 we have represented the eight key information actions as a cycle, although it is obvious that all information does not go through each of the stages in turn. However we can say that information comes to us either by being *received* (an e-mail message for example), *retrieved* (looking up a telephone number in an address book, for example) or *created* (we write a note to someone). Then information can be *changed* (updating a diary entry or an address in a phone book), used to *make a decision* (the flight information that Robert gets from the travel company helps him to make a decision about his travel arrangements) or *communicated* (Robert communicates the details of the flight to the research administrator so he can confirm them). Figure 3.1 represents this complete cycle, ending in information either being *stored* (where it can be retrieved or communicated again) or *discarded* (we do not need it). The smaller diagrams show the possibilities for the key actions of change, decision and communicate. We can see that, although information can be used in a number of ways, the key actions apply at different stages in the information's life.

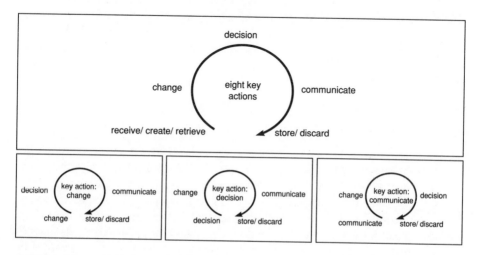

Figure 3.1 The eight key information actions

The eight key information actions allow us to become aware of the way that information is used and, as we will see later, to understand the relationship between information and the forms it appears in. As we will also see later, the eight key information actions are important because they show that information can be managed at each stage of the cycle in different ways, and that different technologies have different abilities to manage information.

By changing the ways we deal with information – how we receive, create, retrieve, change, make a decision, communicate, store and discard – we have a powerful way of making sure that we manage information effectively.

■ Some other perspectives on information

The practical approach to managing personal information we outline in this book is based on much research about the nature of information. We will look quickly at these perspectives to show you some different ways that information has been understood. Our point here is that, while these are all valuable approaches, none of them really gets to grips with the *practical problems* people experience and which we deal with in this book. The perspectives we will look at are (1) *theoretical* – information theory ; (2) *organisational* – management science ; (3) *technological* – information science; and (4) *human* – cognitive psychology.

■ Information theory

Information theory (also known as 'communication theory') was developed by Claude Shannon at the Bell Telephone Company research laboratories in the USA in the 1940s and 1950s. It is a mathematical model of the flow of information which formed the basis for the development of modern communication systems where the aim is to send information at a high speed and volume. We mention information theory because it has often been taken quite literally – as applying to all kinds of information – and this has often meant a very 'mechanistic' view of information. Yet it does not really relate to what people do *practically* with information.

■ Management science

What has come to be known as management science deals with information used for decision making. Management science was developed to deal with the use of resources during the Second World War, producing models for the efficient management of projects. Later, businesses world-wide adopted this approach, in the form of 'operations research' (OR) and applied it to tasks such as marketing, advertising and finance. In 1953 the Institute of Management Sciences was founded and, by 1980, management science was widely used in marketing, finance, public services, information systems and research and development.

In the 1980s management science was influenced by Japanese manufacturing techniques, which suggested looking at an entire system rather than just the 'fine-tuning' of a system. For example, it was found that inventories of materials in manufacturing could be reduced to 'just-in-time' (JIT) levels by changing the way production-line machines worked. Management science also began to include the idea of 'quality': 'total quality control' (TQC) suggests that, to work more effectively, different parts of a company need to communicate and collaborate.

Although management science has been an important business tool, we can see that it does not provide a 'personal' perspective on information. Even though management science can help manage information effectively at the corporate level, individual workers in a business often have little or no say in the ways it happens and the technique does not really help them manage their personal information effectively.

■ Information science

'Information science' is the study of the way in which information can be processed. The emphasis in information science is on human information processing and links up with research in sciences such as biology, physics, computer science, sociology, psychology, and library and information science. Although computer technology has had a great impact on information science, about 50 per cent of all workers in the USA today are in involved in information processing, with or without the aid of computers. One aim of information science is to increase our understanding of the way information is generated, stored and used.

The information scientist compares alternative ways of making information available: for example, by sophisticated indexes of information, or by developing new tools to improve the retrieval and processing of information using computers.

Information science means of course the greater use of computers, especially in the searching of computer databases of information scattered around the globe. For example, libraries (which used to be places where books were stored) now house all kinds of information – access to other libraries is gained by using networks or by the storing of electronic information on CD-Rom, for example.

■ Cognitive psychology

Psychologists basically try to understand why people act the way they do. One thing that psychologists have investigated is how information is stored in and retrieved from our memories. They have tried to find the answers to problems such as how people interpret sights and sounds as meaningful or how they store memories of what has happened to them. A branch of psychology known as 'cognitive psychology' looks in detail at our memory and how we store and retrieve information.

Research has found out that people have different types of memory: a 'short-term memory' that stores sights and sounds for a very short time; a slightly longer-term memory that allows you to store, say, someone's telephone number when they tell you it; and a 'long-term memory' that seems to store things indefinitely. Memory in everyday life is not mostly memorisation of things like telephone numbers: it also involves what things *mean*. Recent research has shown that people are 'active organisers' of information who do not simply soak up information, but try and give some structure to it (for example, the 'chunking' of telephone numbers into groups of two and three digits so that we can remember them easily).

Cognitive psychologists also look at questions such as 'what are the limits of human memory and why doesn't it always work properly?' Most people have experienced the 'tip of the tongue' phenomenon (knowing that they remember the name of a friend without actually being able to say it); when someone else says it, we can instantly remember it. The use of what psychologists call 'cues' is known as the 'recognition/recall phenomenon' and demonstrates that, in trying to remember something, we should have as many cues as possible. 'Mnemonics' (or memory aids) are simple cues which help us remember. For example, a mnemonic for remembering the order of the colours of the spectrum (red, orange, yellow, green, blue, indigo, violet) is the sentence *Richard of York gains battles in vain*. The reason why this works is that the sentence – which actually means something – is much more memorable than the order of the colours (which have no real meaning).

Personal information management is based to a large extent on the way our memories work. If people remember information by organising it better and by understanding it, then one way to become better at managing information is to give it structure.

CHAPTER 4

'Information overload' and information management 're-engineering'

■ Information overload

We have already identified 'information overload' – too much information to deal with in the time available – as one of the most important problems facing professionals today. Many articles and academic research papers have investigated this problem and suggested that one of the major reasons why people are overloaded is the massive growth in the use of information technology. In most companies, computer systems hold the business together – from computer systems which manage our office telephone networks, through those that control and track finances, to computers used for functions like stock control or purchasing.

For the individual, too, information technology is important. Even if people do not have access to e-mail or voice mail, most people experience the effects of information technology. Much of the mail which hits our doormat (for example invitations to apply for credit cards) is the result of the analysis of data on our credit rating and spending patterns. In fact, it is not quite true to say that it is only *computers* which have resulted in information overload. A lot of our information comes in the form of paper documents (letters, journals or newspapers) and it is more accurate to say that *information technology* might be to blame, rather than just computers. This is because computers are only one of the technologies we have to deal with – another being communications technology. The effect is that technologies such as computers and communications 'converge' to supply us with information and ways of dealing with it. In the scenario below we can see the effects of this convergence of information technologies and how they result in information overload.

John, the senior manager of the research group we saw earlier, does the same thing every morning he arrives in his office. First he connects to his e-mail server on his desktop personal computer. In his in-tray on the e-mail server are lists of messages. Some of these are new arrivals and some remain in his in-tray from the previous day. The e-mail messages range from invitations to attend conferences, through more long-term personal correspondence with colleagues around the world, to messages from his colleagues just down the corridor. As he is reading his e-mail, his secretary comes in with the day's paper mail, along with reports on the telephone log of incoming calls from yesterday, fax messages and documents for the day's meetings and events. Some of the mail and calls John's secretary deals with on his behalf, and some are marked for John's attention. John also has a private fax line connected to his PC which stores incoming faxes on confidential projects. He also has a private voice mail line which accepts and stores messages which are not handled by his secretary. His cellular phone also has voice mail for when he cannot have the telephone turned on (in meetings, for example). His pager sits in his coat pocket. The mail also contains a pile of trade and professional weeklies and journals to read. All of this before 9.30 am!

▌Changing (or 're-engineering') your approach to information management

The above scenario does not illustrate an exceptional situation. Many professionals deal with this volume of information and more. It is not surprising, then, that many professionals find themselves slipping into a situation where work is dealt with later and later, and information piles up into an unmanageable mess. This means that a great proportion of professionals' time is spent 'fire-fighting' – simply managing to deal with only the smallest proportion of essential and most urgent items. Others are left to wait for a time when they can deal with them.

We have suggested that you will need to develop a personal information management strategy or PIM Strategy. In a while we will look at the details of developing and maintaining this strategy, but for now it should be obvious that developing and implementing a strategy means *changing what you do in a systematic way*. We would like to suggest that the way you should think about this is as a kind of 're-engineering'. In developing and implementing a PIM strategy you will be *re-engineering how you manage your information*. 'Re-engineering' suggests a very systematic, controlled and planned change to the way you manage your information.

The term 're-engineering' might be familiar from an approach to changing the way organisations work known as 'business process re-engineering' (BPR). There are many management gurus who have developed approaches to BPR, the most familiar being Michael Hammer and James Champey in their book *Re-engineering the Corporation* (Hammer and Champey, 1994). BPR is essentially about changing the way businesses work by looking at the *processes* that businesses use – anything from providing a customer with a quotation to ordering new stock for the assembly of a motor car. The focus is on the processes that need to be changed, and it is a very similar approach to the way in which you will need to change what you do in developing your own PIM strategy.

■ 'Information re-engineering goals' and their benefits

There is no point in changing, or re-engineering, unless you have some goals to achieve and there are concrete benefits in achieving them. There are several information re-engineering goals:

1. make your information more accessible;
2. streamline the way you deal with information;
3. remove 'islands' of information; and
4. reduce your information overload.

The benefits of achieving these goals will be (1) to improve your personal effectiveness; (2) to improve the effectiveness of your team or colleagues; and (3) to increase your feeling of satisfaction or 'congruence'. We will briefly discuss each of these in turn.

■ Make your information more accessible

One of the problems with much of our information is that it is often difficult to retrieve easily. This can mean knowing you received a document, but not being able to find it, or mislaying e-mail messages you know you have read (telephone numbers often create a searching expedition, for example). Information is only useful if you can gain access to it and are able to take the seven key actions we described earlier.

■ Streamline the way you deal with information

Managing your information does not only mean making it more accessible. It also means ensuring that any piece of information is dealt with in an efficient manner, of which the first stage is storage. We will suggest that the storage part of the cycle is one of the most important stages. It will determine how effective your information management is. Storage can mean where on your desk information sits, where it is filed, what medium it is in or when you deal with it.

■ Remove islands of information

The phrase 'islands of information' was first coined in the context of the work of information management in corporations that we discussed earlier. Essentially an 'island of information' is created by information not being able to be linked to other information. This is obvious if you think of an organisation where an e-mail system of one department differs from that of another department, so that workers are unable to exchange information easily. Information in these departments effectively becomes an 'island'. However the concept also applies individuals: many professionals have bought 'electronic organisers' (which we will discuss later) to use as personal note takers or personal diaries. The problems of entering and retrieving information from the organiser (it does not plug into a printer or into your desk-based PC) means that you effectively have an island of information which can cause you problems.

■ Reduce your information overload

Information overload, as we discussed earlier, is a key problem for all professionals. The development of new forms of information communication and storage means that we are bombarded every day by many different types of information, only some of which will be relevant to our needs. In order to combat this problem, know what information you need and, more importantly, what information you do not need.

■ Improve your personal effectiveness

We suggest that, by improving information accessibility and information management, and reducing information overload, you will be able to become more effective, not just more efficient. Part of being more effective is to have clearly thought-out goals and know what information you need. If you receive six professional journals in the mail, but only two are appropriate and useful, do not spend any time reading the other four.

■ Improve the effectiveness of your team or colleagues

Most professionals' work involves teamwork in one form or another. It seems obvious that, if a member of a team becomes more effective, then team effectiveness also increases. This does not simply mean doing things faster (which may of course have an overall negative effect on team effectiveness) but on doing things '*smarter*' – working flexibly, managing information and communicating appropriately.

■ Increase your satisfaction (or 'congruence')

Finally, to use a term borrowed from Anthony Robbins in his book *Unlimited Power* (1988), managing personal information effectively gives a certain intangible 'feel' to the way that you work. Because you will be less prone to information overload, you will find that your time (perhaps using time management tools and techniques) can be better structured to leave time for other, perhaps home-based, activities.

Related re-engineering techniques: time management, conceptual tools and thinking

The techniques we will look at in this book are closely related to some other approaches which win to enable people to 're-engineer' themselves at work or in their personal lives. Although there are many, perhaps the most important are time management, conceptual tools, thinking and getting organised.

■ Time management

We have already mentioned time management, its relationship to information management and its development in the 1980s. In his excellent books on personal development and leadership, Stephen R. Covey looks at the ways in which people can become more effective managers of their time. Covey's ideas are much broader than simple time management but essentially his approach is to look at the ways in which we spend our time, and particularly the mix of work, personal relationships and relaxation.

The most important of Covey's ideas is the *time management matrix* (Table 4.1), which describes the activities and tasks we can perform with our time. Covey says that, to become more effective, we must move away from activities which are not important to our long-term goals (unimportant activities such as interruptions and calls, trivia and time-wasting activities) and try to concentrate on those activities that are important but not urgent (long-term planning, professional updating and networking with colleagues). Although he recognises that urgent matters must be dealt with (crises and problems), Covey suggests that spending more time on long-term planning will eventually help remove the need to act in a crisis mode.

What Covey is describing is the well-known *Pareto's Principle*, otherwise known as 'the 80/20 rule'. This says that in most circumstances 80 per cent of the value comes from 20 per cent of the resources. In this case the 80/20 rule says that 20 per cent of the activities generate 80 per cent of the value of your work. Therefore, suggests Covey, you should make sure the effort you make is in the correct 20 per cent. You must also make sure that you do not spend too much time managing the trivial 80 per cent of information to the neglect of the valuable 20 per cent.

Obviously this approach to managing time is an important step in helping people realise their goals, but in itself it is not enough. We suggest that by re-engineering your information management processes you can achieve complementary benefits by moving towards dealing with more long-term issues, rather than fire-fighting crises and urgent problems.

Table 4.1 The time–management matrix

	Urgent	Not urgent
Important	Crises, problems	Planning, long-term projects
Not important	Interruptions, calls	Trivia, time-wasting

Source: Adapted from Covey (1989).

■ Conceptual tools

A second key 'personal re-engineering' technique is that of conceptual toolmaking, described in the book *Conceptual Toolmaking* by Jerry Rhodes (1991). Rhodes' approach is to suggest that like physical tools we can develop a set of 'conceptual tools' which enable us primarily to solve problems and understand events. Developing conceptual tools is a way of getting some advantage for the user to help in solving problems. In a sense, the concept of 'managing personal information' is a kind of conceptual tool which, if applied well, results in an advantage for the user.

■ Thinking

Another well-known re-engineering technique is that of Edward de Bono, who focuses on 'thinking' itself. In his many books (such as the *Masterthinker's Handbook*, 1985) de Bono looks at strategies which can help people become better thinkers and to 're-engineer' their thought processes. Although there are many of these 'masterthinking' techniques, de Bono makes some key points in the opening chapter of the *Masterthinker's Handbook* which equally apply to personal information management:

- *You have to want to do it* Learning to think, like developing conceptual tools, and like managing your personal information, requires that you are committed to changing your current practices. This is why we call the process of managing personal information a form of re-engineering.
- *You have to focus on it* Improving your personal information management will not happen by itself. It is not something that you can set off and then expect to happen. It requires your continued attention to ensure that the process of re-engineering actually takes place.

- *You have to set some time aside for it* Of course, paying attention means you must set some time aside for it. That is why, in the chapter on your PIM strategy, we suggest that you spend certain periods of time engaging in your personal re-engineering to manage information.
- *You have to have a strategy* It is obvious that you need to have some defined strategy to manage your personal information. Simply doing *anything* will not work.
- *You have to practise* Again, this form of personal re-engineering is something you are not used to and, as with any skill, you need to practise it in order to improve. Later we look at ways in which you can practise effectively.

■ Getting organised

One thing we will emphasise throughout this book is the need to be *organised* in managing personal information. The approach of ensuring that people are better organised is of course one which many books have dealt with. Essentially these approaches suggest that you should remove 'clutter' from your life by 'sorting' information. For example, the book *Getting and Staying Organised* by Corrine Livesay (1994) suggests that by being better organised we can increase *efficiency* (the time taken to process information or perform a task) and *effectiveness* (the ability to achieve goals). As we will see later, these two terms, which are sometimes regarded as meaning the same thing, are in fact very different. It is possible to be efficient and ineffective, but difficult to be inefficient and effective at the same time.

Some of the principles which this approach emphasises are:

- *to eliminate the sources of clutter*, ensuring that you have less information to deal with;
- *to analyse sources of clutter*, by keeping records of how many pieces of information (articles, notes, e-mail message and phone calls) you deal with;
- *to pass information on to where it will have the most effect*, if an e-mail message can be better dealt with by a colleague, then pass it on directly;
- *to deal with things immediately*, do not leave information lying around where it will pile up to be dealt with later.

Corrine Livesay gives the example of how to deal with mail: you can either 'junk' it immediately (some envelopes announce themselves as junk advertising mail); discard it after opening (some mail, even if it looks valuable, can be discarded after opening); mark it for action (make sure that it will be useful later by attaching a note to tell you what to do with it); or immediately direct it elsewhere (either to a file for later reference or to a colleague for action).

Removing clutter is useful but it is only *part* of the story, and only one part of managing personal information more effectively.

CHAPTER 5

Understanding information management technology

We have so far looked at what information is, what we do with it, and have suggested that you need to 're-engineer' to manage your information better. What we now need to do is look at the *technology* we can use to manage personal information. By 'technology' we mean here not only information technology – such as the telephone, fax machine or e-mail – but also the paper-based technologies which we are most familiar with: diaries, filing cabinets, books and Post-it notes.

Many people will be familiar with some or all of the technologies we will discuss (listed in Table 5.1). Most people will of course use paper-based technologies, such as those listed here, and variants of them. More people will be familiar with some of the huge range of computer software applications which have been around for several years. Fewer people will be familiar with, and use on a regular basis, some of the telecommunications technologies such as pagers and voice mail. An even smaller number will regularly use devices such as 'personal digital assistants' like the Apple *Newton*, or make extensive use of CD-Rom information. Finally, fewer people use computer networks intensively, although the numbers of people joining commercial networks such as *CompuServe*, *Delphi* and *America Online*, and then getting connected to the Internet, is growing rapidly. A 22 per cent increase (to $3.3 billion in revenues) is expected by 1997 in the on-line services market, according to a survey by Dataquest, Inc. (*Investors Business Daily*, 16 August 1995).

Most people are surprised when they recognise just how many of these technologies they actually use in the course of their professional lives. Some of the scenarios we have provided suggest how some people use them when performing one task or in the course of a working day. But, even if these technologies are used, fewer people actually have a strategy for using them. Most offices and professionals equip themselves with many technologies but it is the technology that determines how it is used, rather than the users of the technology. You may suggest that you might like to receive an e-mail message rather than a fax, or a fax message rather than a telephone call, or that you would prefer to make notes

Table 5.1   A range of information management technologies

Computer software	Spreadsheets
	Databases
	Word processors
	Personal organisers
	Calendars
	E-mail
Computer hardware	Personal digital assistants
	CD-Rom
	Scanners
Computer networks	Internet
	CompuServe
	Delphi
Telecommunications	Pagers
	Fax
	Voice mail
	Cellphones
	Office phones
Paper	Files
	Post-it notes
	Wall calendars
	To-do lists
	Books
	Magazines
	Time management systems
	Calendars

on a word processor rather than handwriting them, but beyond looking at the individual technologies themselves most professionals have no overall strategy for managing their information using these technologies.

We have discussed the possibility that you can 're-engineer' your information management to become more effective. Any strategy for doing this must also take into account the ways in which the various information management technologies can be used most effectively. In this chapter we will take a look at a framework for understanding and managing information technologies which will be of practical use in understanding some of the other techniques described in this book, before moving on, in the next two chapters, to look at each technology in detail.

A framework for information management technologies: the 'five technology potentials'

If we look back at the 'eight key information actions' (receive, retrieve, create, change, make decisions, communicate, store, discard) we can begin to see how each technology plays a part in managing personal information. First we can map the eight key information actions onto the technologies themselves and look at the way each kind of technology enables the eight key information actions. Table 5.2 shows what kinds of technologies support each of the key information actions.

While some aspects of all of the eight key information actions can be found in all technologies, we are looking at the *primary* quality before classifying which of the key information actions it enables (we have assumed for convenience that *discard* is something all of the technologies will allow). One thing that we can see immediately from Table 5.2 is that there are many forms in which information is *stored* (this of course accounts for 'information overload'). Technology provides so many ways of storing information that we end up with many different types of stored information. We can also see that there are many ways of *receiving* information, mostly using communications devices. As we saw earlier, the information cycle starts with receiving some information and ends with the storage or discarding of information.

We will not work through Table 5.2 in detail, partly because we will be looking at technologies in detail in the next two chapters, and partly because there are no exact and clear-cut properties of each of the technologies. What we would like you to understand from the table is that *different technologies provide different possibilities for managing information.*

■ Five 'technology potentials'

The next step is to look at other ways in which information and information management technologies are important. We suggest that there are, essentially, five key concepts which we can apply to information management technologies. These are concerned with the 'potential' of those technologies to help us manage information and to perform the eight key information actions.

1. *Information flow*: does the technology have the potential to allow information to flow easily? Ensuring that information flows is important to make sure that information reaches the right person at the right time.
2. *Information breadth*: does the technology provide the capacity to manage different kinds of information? Ensuring that you have a range of information is essential if decisions are to be made appropriately.
3. *Information depth*: does the technology provide the capacity to manage detailed information? Ensuring that you have the most detailed picture of a situation or problem is important in planning and anticipating.

Table 5.2 Technologies and the eight key information actions

		Receive	Retrieve	Create	Change	Decision	Communicate	Store
Software	Spreadsheets		▲	▲	▲	▲		▲
	Databases		▲	▲	▲	▲		▲
	Word processors			▲	▲			▲
	Organisers				▲	▲		▲
	Calendars		▲			▲		▲
	E-mail programs	▲		▲			▲	▲
Hardware	PDAs		▲					▲
	CD-Roms		▲					▲
Networks	Internet	▲	▲				▲	
	CompuServe	▲	▲				▲	
	Delphi	▲	▲				▲	
Communications	Pagers	▲	▲				▲	
	Fax	▲		▲			▲	
	Voice mail	▲	▲	▲			▲	▲
	Cellphones	▲					▲	
	Telephones	▲					▲	
Paper	Files		▲					▲
	Post-its	▲		▲		▲	▲	▲
	Wall calendars					▲		▲
	To do lists			▲	▲	▲		▲
	Books	▲						
	Magazines	▲						
	Time managers					▲		▲
	Calendars					▲		▲

4. *Information accessibility*: does the technology provide the capacity to gain access to information easily? This is crucial to managing time and activities.
5. *Information interconnectedness*: does the technology allow information to be interconnected? Ensuring that you can link up various pieces of information may be important in solving a particular problem or completing a project.

If we look again at the various information management technologies, we can see how each of them rates in terms of the five technology potentials. In Table 5.3 '1' means that the technology has a low rating, '2' a medium rating and '3' a high rating for one of the five potentials. This of course is a simplistic way of looking at information management technologies, but it allows us to draw a number of conclusions:

Table 5.3   The five technology potentials

		Flow	*Breadth*	*Depth*	*Accessibility*	*Interconnectedness*
Software	Spreadsheets	1	1	3	2	3
	Databases	1	3	3	2	3
	Word processors	1	2	2	2	2
	Organisers	2	3	1	1	3
	Calendars	1	3	1	1	2
	E-mail programs	3	3	2	3	1
Hardware	PDAs	2	3	1	3	3
	CD-Roms	1	3	3	3	3
Networks	Internet	3	3	2	3	3
Communications	Pagers	3	1	1	3	1
	Fax	2	2	2	2	1
	Voice mail	3	2	2	3	1
	Cellphones	2	2	3	3	1
	Telephones	2	2	3	3	1
Paper	Files	1	3	3	3	2
	Post-its	3	1	1	3	1
	Wall calendars	1	3	1	3	3
	To do lists	3	3	2	3	3
	Books	1	3	3	3	2
	Time managers	2	3	2	3	3
	Calendars	1	3	1	3	1

1. Communication technologies have a high capacity to realise each of the information potentials. They have the most potential to provide for the *flow* of information and *accessibility* of information.
2. Computer software provides *breadth* and *depth* of information effectively and has the ability to *interconnect* information.
3. Paper technologies provide for *breadth* and *accessibility* of information but have less potential for promoting the *flow* of information than some others.

There are many more conclusions we might draw from the ways in which different technologies rate on the five potentials, but perhaps the most important is that *appropriate technologies must be used for dealing with different kinds of information.*

In the next chapter we will look at some of those technologies and provide some practical help and guidance on choosing appropriate technologies.

CHAPTER 6

Personal information technologies: advantages and disadvantages

In this chapter and the next two we will look at personal information management products, both paper-based and electronic. We will spend quite a lot of time looking at computer-based products for the simple reason that their usefulness is continually improving, especially if they are understood and used correctly. We will look at their advantages and disadvantages, suggest ways to evaluate their appropriateness for you, and help you decide whether they are worth investing the time, money and effort to learn and use. Finally we will start to help you to define your own PIM strategy.

How to choose personal information products

Sometimes too many options can be more difficult than too few. This sums up the situation facing the business professional today who is looking for new computer software, personal organisation products or scheduling products. Computer stores are lined with hundreds of different software packages and gadgets that promise to make life easier and allow you to perform your work efficiently. It is the same situation in office supply stores. The question of course is: how do you choose between the options, especially when your time is limited and valuable?

The first step to choosing personal information products and developing your PIM strategy is to *analyse your needs*. Rather than investigating every possible product or software option, you should begin with an idea of what is going to work best for you. Do you want to use a computer and attempt to put as much of your information as possible on your notebook computer for maximum mobility? Or do you feel much more comfortable with paper and definitely do not want to take the time and effort to purchase and learn to use a computer?

We will assume, in this chapter and the two following, that you have a clear set of goals about what you wish to achieve, in terms both of your business activities and of your personal goals. These are of course essential (as many businesses have found out to their cost) if you are to define ways of moving forward. We will mention 'your goals' and 'ways of helping achieve your goals' and we assume that one of your goals is 'to become more effective and efficient', which is one of the driving ideas behind the whole concept of personal information management: managing information to make your contribution more effective, and to make you more comfortable with the information you need to manage. (The process of setting goals is of course itself very valuable. The books mentioned in Chapter 4, by Steven Covey and Anthony Robbins, are excellent tools to help you to develop your goals.)

■ How information is stored and managed

In the 1990s there are essentially two basic formats that hold information: paper and electronic. 'Electronic information' is information stored in computers – which amounts to information which is reduced to a digital representations – a series of 1s and 0s ('bits') written into a computer memory, either in the form of a 'Read-Only-Memory' (ROM) or on a computer diskette, which usually contains around 1Mb (a 'megabyte' or 1 million bytes) of information which can be erased and rewritten.

Paper is one of the oldest and the most common carriers of information; after a few brief lessons around the age of two, we inherently understand how to use paper. Electronic information is a relatively new development (dating from around 1940, when the first specialised computer systems were developed). This is the most unfamiliar and newest form of information. Professionals in all fields have only recently started routinely to use electronic information, using personal computers to store and retrieve information, or to gain access to more sophisticated sources of information over computer networks or over the Internet.

Our collective lack of experience with electronic information means that it is not surprising that many people experience problems using it. The rapid introduction of computers into the workplace, with little or no training, means that people are often confused and sometimes a little frightened of electronic information. And of course, since we do not have the vast amount of familiarity and experience that we do with paper-based information – even if we are computer-literate – we have no systematic strategies for storing or retrieving electronic information.

As we will discuss in more detail later, developing your own PIM strategy means making the very practical first decision of whether you want to use predominantly paper or electronic information. Of course, many professionals will need both types of information (official paper records will always need to be stored for some important purposes) but making a first decision on what you will use predominantly will be very helpful. This decision will also help you choose what sorts of tools you will need to use to work with that information.

Until computers become as easy to use as paper (which may be some time) and until the entire globe goes on-line (which may be even longer) many people will experience difficulties and frustration with electronic information and the computer-based tools used to manage it. It will be some time before we have computers that are as easy to use as those on 'Star Trek: The Next Generation', for example, where all inputs and outputs are performed by speaking to the computer. Instead of typing commands, the user asks the computer questions and the computer responds verbally; if the computer needs clarification of a request, it asks for one. No cryptic comments to understand. Paper is never seen on 'Star Trek'. When a staff member turns in a report to the captain, it is handed to him on a computer disk.

Although the intelligent speech-based computer is a long way from being a reality, many thought that the introduction of computers to business would result in 'the paperless office'. That has not happened, even though more and more transactions can be made using computers (with technologies such as 'electronic data exchange' or EDI, where orders and payments can be made completely electronically) and more information can be reduced to bits (using digital scanners, fax machines and voice mail systems). It will be a long time before paper can be eliminated from our lives completely.

There are many advantages to using electronic information and computer-based tools to manage it. However there are also decisions that should be made before deciding to work predominantly with electronic information. For some people the decision is easy – they are excited about the computing power currently available and eagerly look forward to each new technological development. Other people do not like computers, do not understand how to use them and are afraid of them (which mostly amounts to being afraid of what happens when they break down). Anyone who has difficulty overcoming that fear will gain less of an advantage from using electronic information and computers as they will spend time creating numerous back-ups of information, mostly on paper.

Before deciding what form of information you predominantly want to use, we consider both the advantages and disadvantages of paper and electronic information.

■ Advantages of paper

- Easily understood; people have been familiar with paper since childhood. The common tool for storing paper is the filing cabinet. It was first introduced in 1893 and, while it has changed in appearance, has essentially retained the same functions.
- No technological 'glitches' (unless you lose it).
- Most information is still contained on paper: memos, letters, brochures, newspapers and magazines.
- Paper is still the common denominator: where people have incompatible electronic information systems (different computers, different networks or different equipment) it is used as the common medium of information exchange.
- It is easy to transport information in small amounts.
- There is (little or) no learning curve.

■ Disadvantages of paper

- A large amount of information becomes difficult to manage. For example, retrieving information quickly can be a problem unless you have elaborate filing and indexing systems.
- Information that needs to be incorporated into an existing paper document often requires that the entire document be recreated.
- Considerable storage space is required.
- A large volume of paper is difficult to transport. An equivalent amount of information on the computer would easily fit on a 3.5 inch diskette.

■ Advantages of electronic information

- Large amounts of information can be stored very efficiently.
- Information can be retrieved with comparative ease and quickly (using a key-word search, for example).
- Information is transportable. Using a portable computer you can carry all of your files around with you; using a remote access program, information can be retrieved from a remote location.
- Names and contact information (one of the most common types of information used by professionals) can be stored and accessed much more easily and in greater volume. For example, data from 500 business cards can easily be stored on your computer in a database program. The file can also be stored on a floppy diskette or on a notebook computer and can be transported with you, or a printout can be made easily. Contrast that with trying to transport a Rolodex with 500 business cards. Even putting the information into a personal organiser is not a workable solution, as the book will probably be straining at the seams.
- 'Navigation by description' is possible with electronic information. This means that you can look around for the information you need by searching for descriptions and notes added to information.

■ Disadvantages of electronic information

- Cost: although the cost of each individual bit of information is infinitesimally small, the practical costs of electronic information can be great, since you need the computer-based tools and utilities to store and access the information. For someone trying to manage a struggling small business, or a corporation attempting to reduce expenditure, the cost can be a disadvantage unless it can be shown that long-term costs will be reduced by increasing efficiency and effectiveness.
- Efficiency is not automatic: many people think that using electronic information and purchasing a computer will automatically make them more efficient and able to accomplish more. While the use of computers to deal with electronic information *may* result in efficiency and effectiveness, it does not guarantee it. Experience and problem-solving skills must be added to the equation before electronic information (and the use of computers) truly increases efficiency. The most productive companies tend to spend less per employee on management information systems (MIS) when compared to companies with average productivity. Also it has been found that companies with the highest profits

tend to have the most administrators per knowledge worker (Henkoff, 1991, p.73).

- Time investment: a statement commonly heard in many offices is, 'I don't have *time* to learn how to use the computer!' However, if a computer is to be used to manage electronic information, the user must expect to spend a significant amount of time learning and becoming familiar with the computer. The time required may increase as more software programs are added (even though users will become more expert at learning the features and problems of new software).

- Learning curve: the learning curve when using computers is relatively steep. In order to become an expert user who can get the maximum advantage from the electronic information managed by a computer, you will always have to solve problems by consulting books and help menus. Very often the source of the problem will not be readily identifiable, and trouble-shooting must be done. This requires time and patience.

- Different problem-solving skills are required: while computers offer great advantages, they also have the potential to create difficult and complex problems. Modems that do not connect, printers that do not print and files that for some strange reason cannot be opened are all everyday problems that delay the accomplishment of your work. The reason for any of these problems may be simple, or it may be a complex problem requiring extensive knowledge and problem-solving skills. Few professionals want to be expert computer users – they just want to get their work done. They are often forced into the role of an 'expert' by having to learn strange and arcane facts about their computer's internal operation. This can be frustrating, and encourages people to engage in 'workarounds' – making printouts of everything – and thus reducing the benefits that the technology produces.

- Computers do not eliminate paper: as we noted earlier, if you do decide to use mostly electronic information and computer-based tools to manage it, you still must deal with paper. For instance, there are many software programs that can help you produce expense account reports or manage your finances. As good as these programs are, you must still deal with paper. Most employers expect to see original receipts for expenses and your financial information still arrives on paper in the form of bills or statements. Many companies that have invested a lot of time and money in computer power have noticed that it is not used as effectively as it might be. A CEO of a company quoted in a *Fortune* article noticed that all the information people needed was in the computer system, but employees were making decisions using paper documents. As the system design became more responsive to the needs of employees and not the data-processing department, the computer system was used more often and more effectively (Henkoff, 1991, p.84).

- Computers often do not lend themselves to the full range of our senses: there are many people who rely particularly on *visual* cues to remember where information is. A computer, with its rectangular box, using a text-based interface (such as the MS-DOS or UNIX operating systems) will not help the people who rely on visual cues. Even using more sophisticated 'graphical user interfaces' (GUIs – pronounced 'gooeys'), such as Microsoft Windows or the Apple Macintosh, many users find problems since many of the design features of these systems are at odds with their experience in the real world. For instance, do you look at files through a window, and does your desk really have a wastebasket on it?

- Should this process or task be computerised? Before deciding to use electronic information you must carefully determine whether it is even appropriate to use the information electronically and use a computer to manage it. If the process or the information you want to computerise does not add value, then it is not worth doing. Then the appropriate action is not to automate, but to stop doing that work.

Looking at these advantages and disadvantages might make you feel that the decision as to what kind of information you want to use and what technology you want to manage it with is an elementary one. Elementary it may be, but it is still crucial. For example, a colleague related this story to us. A friend of his neglected to ask himself whether he wanted to spend the effort it would take to begin using a personal computer. He purchased an expensive computer system and paid a computer consultant to set it up. In addition to word processing and other standard software, he decided that he should use a contact manager software program to keep track of business cards obtained at networking events. He had even hired someone to set up the contact manager software and type in the information. At this stage everything should have been perfect. But it was not. He was not certain if he liked the contact management software, and refused to learn it. As he continued to collect other business cards, they began to pile up on his desk. He asked us what to do with the business cards. When we suggested putting the cards into his contact manager program, he balked at the suggestion. He did not really like that contact manager program, which is a good program with a large market share. Instead of using it, he thought another software package would be the answer to his problem. While he had very good tools in place to help him manage his information, he would not use them. This was a case where the computer alone did not create any efficiency because no time was invested in learning to use it.

In fact, deciding whether to use a computer is similar to deciding where to go on holiday. To decide where you want to go, it is necessary to make some basic decisions about what you want to do and stick with that plan. Otherwise you will spend your entire holiday wishing you were doing something else or, worse, trying to do everything and ending up exhausted at the conclusion. Often personal information management 'non-strategies' are like this. Looking again at computer systems, we may think one word processing program is perfect. Then we hear about another one that is supposed to be perfect and begin using it. If we want to retrieve a document, we have to remember in what software program it was created. Frequently changing software adds to the confusion. This is because the commands to perform different functions are not the same and we spend time relearning what we already knew with another program. Some planning and consideration of your needs beforehand will help with this situation.

A further 'non-strategy' is switching databases. We decide that a new database will be perfect and we begin to use it, only to discard it later because it is not easy to understand. Instead of investing the time to learn it, we look for something better. The new database is purchased because it does one function well that was a problem in the other database. However the second database does not do several other things well. While one problem has been solved, others have been created.

CHAPTER 7

Computer software and hardware products

As we said in the previous chapter, there are thousands of beneficial and interesting software applications which can help with your PIM strategy. However all but the most sophisticated computer users should focus their attention on just a few software applications that will work best for them. Trying to learn and incorporate too many programs at one time is a recipe for certain failure.

When deciding what software package to use, it is helpful to keep in mind that no package is perfect. You should therefore determine what your crucial needs are and then test each package to see how it handles them. The best program should be the one you decide to use. Before looking at the various categories of software programs, it is important to make a distinction between two separate functions of software programs: *information production* and *information storage*.

Let us take a look at the production aspect of software. A word processing program assists you in 'producing' information in the form of proposals and letters. Spreadsheet programs also assist with 'producing' financial analyses. Other types of programs that are production-oriented are presentation programs that create slide shows or outlines for presentations, or a program that produces your income tax returns. Other types of software with production capabilities are *résumé* programs or ones that create greeting cards or signs. The amount of information stored in these programs is very small. The only information they contain is the information that was provided in order to create the final product.

Software packages can also provide an information *storage* function. Word processing documents, once they are created, can also be easily and effectively stored. Other information such as e-mail or scanned documents can also be stored in a word processing program. The same concept applies to spreadsheets. By creating appropriate directories, you can group similar spreadsheets for a certain category or client and, as past information is needed, it can be retrieved within seconds and alterations made and a new version saved under a new name. The spreadsheet, in addition to its production capabilities, also provides an efficient and effective system in which to store information.

Both word processors and accounting packages have an approximately equal number of production and information storage capabilities. Spreadsheets are more oriented towards production, but other programs are more oriented towards information storage. For instance, the presentation package produces a slide show for a presentation, but its information storage capabilities are limited. While you can store a slide show in the package, it is not possible to store the background information that supported the creation of the slide show in that package. That information will probably be found on paper or in another software program.

While this may seem like an unimportant distinction, the failure to make it often leads people down the wrong path. For instance, a production-oriented software program will not help you manage information and decrease the volume of paper you have to keep and manage, but a program that has more information storage capabilities will provide that function. While no software programs are exclusively production- or storage-oriented, it is useful to look at their primary qualities before deciding which ones will help you manage your papers and information.

Below we describe different categories of software packages. While there are many different brands of software you can buy for any task, the general characteristics of the software remains the same, and the discussion below focuses on those characteristics. The discussion is purposely not brand-specific, but some popular types of software programs are listed at the end of each discussion as examples. Use the tables to help you decide if the software will be worth buying and using. As you look at these descriptions, decide if each software category provides a function that you need. While all software has its individual benefits, it is important that you choose the software that provides the benefits you need. Otherwise the old saying, 'Too much of a good thing is bad', will apply.

■ Spreadsheets

■ What spreadsheets do

Spreadsheets essentially 'crunch numbers'. They perform complex calculations in a matter of seconds and can let you see the results of your calculations. Such things as a departmental budget, financial analysis and a proposal for product expenditure are some of the things that spreadsheets do effectively.

■ Advantages

The results of changing one variable in a set of calculations can be seen within seconds, eliminating the need to spend a considerable amount of time doing calculations. Graphs illustrating financial figures can be produced easily. Statistical calculations such as linear regressions can be done.

■ Information storage or production?

Spreadsheets are rated 5 in Table 7.1, as they have a slightly stronger production function than an information storage function. While spreadsheets can store financial information efficiently, much additional financial information is probably stored in other paper-based formats or computer software packages.

Table 7.1 Spreadsheets: information storage or production?

Storage						Production
1	2	3	4	5	6	7

■ Should you use a spreadsheet?

That depends. How often do you need to calculate numbers? If you frequently need to do complex financial calculations, then a spreadsheet will be useful. However, if you see yourself using a spreadsheet only once or twice a year for a simple departmental budget that involves no more than adding several numbers, a spreadsheet probably is not essential. If you are just becoming familiar with computers, and do not have frequent need of a spreadsheet, this is a good product to begin using later.

■ Do you really need a spreadsheet?

After considering the above questions, you may have a clear-cut answer to the question of whether you need a spreadsheet. However, if you still are not sure, try answering the questions below.

Add the numbers in Table 7.2 and then average the results. A number close to 5 means that the program will require little time or energy, and your learning curve will be small. A number close to 1 means that you will require more effort and your learning curve will be greater. If it is essential that you have this capability, you should go ahead and get the software.

Table 7.2 Do you really need a spreadsheet?

	A lot				A little
Time to learn	1	2	3	4	5
Energy to understand	1	2	3	4	5
Learning curve	1	2	3	4	5

Average score _____

■ Popular spreadsheets

Microsoft *Excel*, Lotus *123*, Borland *Quattro Pro*.

■ Accounting software

■ What accounting software does

These packages allow you to do your own bookkeeping. The small businessperson who wishes to save time and pay bills quickly will find these packages immensely helpful. They allow you to enter your cheque payment information, and then print these cheques in no more time than it takes to print an equivalent number of letters. The printed cheques also include space for the mailing address. Using a window envelope allows bills to be paid and mailed within a matter of a few minutes. As the cheque information is keyed in, you also key in which expense category it should be. The real time savings occur at the end of the month, or accounting period, when profit and loss and other reports can be produced by simply clicking your mouse button and waiting for the printout.

■ Advantages

The greatest advantage of these programs is the speed with which cheques can be produced. The other big advantage is that producing your accounting reports requires no other effort than keying in the information for cheques. The reports are developed from that information.

■ Information storage or production?

The accounting package holds nearly all of your financial information, as well as producing cheques and financial reports. These functions occur in equal proportion; that is why it is rated a 4 in Table 7.3.

Table 7.3   Accounting packages: information storage or production?

Storage						*Production*
1	2	3	4	5	6	7

■ Should you use an accounting package?

If you are a small business owner who wants to save money on bookkeeping costs and who wants to pay bills efficiently, this will be an invaluable software tool. If you want to handle your personal finances efficiently and know what your financial status is down to the last penny within a few seconds, this is an efficient way to do it.

■ Do you really need an accounting package?

Table 7.4   Accounting packages: do you really need one?

	A lot				*A little*
Time to learn	1	2	3	4	5
Energy to understand	1	2	3	4	5
Learning curve	1	2	3	4	5

Average score _____

■ Popular packages

MYOB Accounting, *Peachtree Accounting*, Intuit *Quicken* and *Quickbooks*, *DacEasy Accounting*.

■ Billing software

■ What billing software does

These packages let you enter the time spent and work accomplished for your clients. They are particularly suited to people who bill clients on an hourly rate, and who need to rebill clients for expenses incurred on their behalf. You can enter the date, the time spent, who performed the work, an hourly rate and a description of the work that was performed.

■ Advantages

Time spent can be entered as the work is done, thereby allowing each telephone call made, letter written or work produced to be completed with the final act of entering the time. The person doing the work can make the entry in a matter of 10–20 seconds. This has several advantages. First, there is no miscommunication between the person doing the work and the one who is entering the time. Second, the time entry task is completed at the conclusion of the call, when the letter has been written or the work performed. Thus it does not show up on a list of things to do as a separate item. Third, it can be done when the content of what was completed is fresh in your mind. Producing bills at the end of the month then becomes a matter of printing them, with a quick glance to make sure everything is correct. If you do not want to enter the time yourself, it can be dictated and an assistant can do it.

■ Information storage or production?

This type of product is rated 6 in Table 7.5 because it performs mostly a production function. While the time entries are stored for the current billing period, after the bills are produced the time entries are usually no longer accessible. Instead, copies of previous monthly bills must be contained on paper. Historical information and account receivable information are still contained in the program.

Table 7.5 Billing packages: information storage or production?

Storage						Production
1	2	3	4	5	6	7

■ Should you use a billing package?

If you are a lawyer, accountant, consultant or writer who bills clients on an hourly basis, this is a very important software tool. If you do not bill clients by the time spent, a billing package will not be helpful.

■ Do you really need a billing package?

Table 7.6 Do you really need a billing package?

	A lot				A little
Time to learn	1	2	3	4	5
Energy to understand	1	2	3	4	5
Learning curve	1	2	3	4	5

Average score _____

■ Popular package

Timeslips.

■ Word processing

■ What a word processor does

Word processors are one of the most common software programs that people use, and also one of the oldest. Word processors allow you to write letters, memos and documents. After you are finished, you can check the spelling and grammar in your document. If you want another word, word processors typically have a thesaurus. Advanced features let you develop outlines that are automatically renumbered if you add or subtract a point. Mail merge allows you to send personalised letters to many people using the same form letter.

■ Advantages

The advantages of a word processor are numerous. Spell checking, find and replace, cut and copy and the ease with which changes can be made are just some of the features that can make creating documents easier. Another advantage is less obvious: word processors are very efficient as an information manager if they are set up correctly. However people often do not make full use of word processing packages as an information manager. How to use a word processor as an information manager will be discussed in further detail later.

■ Information storage or production?

A word processor is rated a 4 in Table 7.7 because everything that it produces can be stored in exactly the same format.

Table 7.7 Word processors: information storage or production?

Storage						*Production*
1	2	3	4	5	6	7

■ Should you use a word processor?

You may not want to use a word processing package if you do not know how to use the computer and if you still have the option of having someone do your typing for you, whether it is your secretary or a secretarial service. To speed the process up, you may want to do your own document creation in order to edit your document as you write, rather than waiting for a new copy to be produced.

■ Do you really need a word processor?

Table 7.8 Word processors: do you really need one?

	A lot				*A little*
Time to learn	1	2	3	4	5
Energy to understand	1	2	3	4	5
Learning curve	1	2	3	4	5

Average score _____

■ Popular products

WordPerfect, Microsoft *Word*, Lotus *Ami Pro*.

■ Databases

■ What databases do

Databases store information about people and companies. They store very small, simple pieces of information, such as names, addresses or telephone numbers. They can also store detailed and complex information about clients' sales history, product ordering and other records. There are in fact several basic types of databases, ranging from the large, complex 'relational' database (which allows you to create complex links and relationships between separate pieces of information) to the small, and more simple, 'flat-file' databases, in which information is stored in simple records, which represent one piece of information at a time, and which are usually more appropriate for personal use. Companies who deal with vast quantities of interrelated information (insurance companies, for example) use complex relational databases.

Database programs can be broken into two major groupings. One is a 'preformatted' database. These are databases that have their structure already set up. 'Fields', areas where information is located, are preset and labelled to indicate clearly where you enter your name, address or fax number. 'Reports', or printouts of information, are also predetermined. You can select different reports such as a telephone list, mailing labels or an address book. While the end-user is able to make some adjustments to the fields, the nature of the program is determined by the way it is programmed. For the user with no special requirements, who is not very comfortable setting up his own database and does not want to spend much time doing it, a preformatted database is a very good option.

■ Advantages of a preformatted database

The strongest advantage of a preformatted database is that it collects small pieces of information, such as telephone numbers, addresses and fax numbers, and puts them all in one place. And, if you wish to send out a mailing to all of your contacts or friends, or invite them to a party, labels can be printed, which saves the task of addressing dozens of envelopes.

■ Information storage or production?

The preformatted database is rated a 2 in Table 7.9 for its information storage capabilities. While it is capable of printing a variety of items, such as lists and mailing labels, its primary function is that of holding information, much of which will never be printed.

Table 7.9 Preformatted databases: information storage or production?

Storage						Production
1	2	3	4	5	6	7

■ Should you use a preformatted databases?

If you like the idea of keeping all of your information on the computer, and if you are prepared to enter the pieces of information as you receive them, this will be a very beneficial product. But if you are nervous about using a computer, or afraid your telephone numbers will be 'lost', it is probably a better idea to stick with your current paper system. If your current paper system is not effective, that is, if you cannot find any telephone number or address within a matter of seconds, then this may be one software package that you should adopt.

■ Do you really need a preformatted database?

Table 7.10 Do you really need a preformatted database?

	A lot				A little
Time to learn	1	2	3	4	5
Energy to understand	1	2	3	4	5
Learning curve	1	2	3	4	5

Average score _____

■ Popular products

Lotus Organiser, Symantec's *Act*, Starfish's *SideKick*, Microsoft *Bob*, *Packrat* by Polaris Software.

■ What does a non-preformatted database do?

A non-preformatted database gives you a 'blank canvas', and you must determine the fields you need, their names, how large they should be and where they should be placed. While you have a maximum amount of flexibility, you also have a development job to do long before you begin entering your data into the program or using it. While these types of databases have become progressively easier to use, they still require solid knowledge to implement and use effectively.

■ Advantages

The advantage of this type of program is that you have maximum flexibility and the ability to design a database that fits your needs precisely. This also is the disadvantage for the new computer user, as designing a database requires a thorough understanding of computers and database operations.

■ Information storage or production?

Table 7.11   Non-preformatted databases: information storage or production?

Storage						*Production*
1	2	3	4	5	6	7

■ Should you use a non-preformatted database?

If you need maximum flexibility, or if you have lots of unique data that cannot fit into a preformatted database, a non-preformatted database is a good tool to use. However this software product, above all other types, demands a certain degree of sophistication.

■ Do you really need a non-preformatted database?

Table 7.12   Do you really need a non-preformatted database?

	A lot				*A little*
Time to learn	1	2	3	4	5
Energy to understand	1	2	3	4	5
Learning curve	1	2	3	4	5

Average score _____

■ Popular products

Microsoft *FoxPro* or *Access*, Lotus *Approach* and Borland's *dBase* or *Paradox*.

▮ Personal organisers/personal information managers (PIMs)

■ What personal organisers do

The popularity of 'time management systems' on paper has prompted many companies to create a version of their paper-based product as software. Essentially these are the same products, delivering the same information, only in a different format. Personal organisers (often called 'personal information managers' or PIMs) have become very popular in the last 10 to 15 years, along with time management classes. Within the last few years, companies producing these products have transferred the same concepts into software programs. The software personal organisers contain the owner's schedule, to-do list, names and numbers and sundry other bits of information. They may also include goals or other planning areas.

■ Advantages

One advantage software personal organisers have over paper organisers is the ability to produce mailing labels or other reports from the data. If you want to do a personalised mailing, you can print labels either from the software or by exporting the data to your word processing software. No additional data entry is required. Software personal organisers also allow you to have a 'clean'-looking organiser. Instead of having lines drawn through cancelled appointments or changed telephone numbers, the on-screen viewing and the printout are clean and uncluttered. If you do want to know when an appointment was cancelled or to look at an old address, that information will be gone, not simply crossed out. (Some programs let you draw a line through a cancelled or completed item, rather than just deleting it.)

■ Information storage or production?

Personal organiser software is rated a 2 in Table 7.13, the same as a for preformatted database, because its primary purpose is to hold information, not to produce reports or mailing labels. While those functions can be performed, they typically will not be done frequently.

Table 7.13   Personal organiser: information storage or production?

Storage						*Production*
1	2	3	4	5	6	7

■ Should you use a personal organiser?

This is one product where putting the information on the computer does not necessarily create huge advantages over a paper system and, if you already have name and address information in another database, the advantages of adopting a computer-based organiser may not be too numerous. If you are out of your office a lot, and do not have a notebook computer that you can take with you, you will need to print out your schedule and telephone numbers, which means you are using paper again.

If you are working in a company that has a networked version of a personal organiser, personal information manager or calendar product, and your work involves many meetings with co-workers, this tool will help facilitate the scheduling of meetings, assuming everyone puts their schedule on the software. If only a few people post their schedule, you are back to paper memos, telephone messages or perhaps e-mail to set up meetings.

■ Do you really need a personal organiser?

Table 7.14   Do you really need a personal organiser?

	A lot				*A little*
Time to learn	1	2	3	4	5
Energy to understand	1	2	3	4	5
Learning curve	1	2	3	4	5

Average score _____

■ Products

Day-Timer *Organiser*, Franklin *Ascend*, T*ime Manager International*, *Priority Manager International*.

■ E-mail programs

■ What e-mail programs do

This software allows you to send and receive electronic mail among co-workers who are connected to the same computer network. For those people who are not part of your computer network, there are other programs that provide e-mail service, such as *MCI Mail*, *Delphi*, *CompuServe*, *America On-Line*, and *Prodigy*.

■ Advantages

One advantage of e-mail is the speed and efficiency with which you can communicate. Responses to messages or questions for co-workers can be composed and sent in a matter of seconds. The communication medium is very informal and quick. It is informal because, unlike the case with a memo or letter, only one brief subject can be addressed in a matter of a few sentences. Writers of other documents may feel compelled to write more to fill up the paper. If you have a typing error in the message, or if your prose is not perfect, those problems are given more latitude than they would be in a paper-based letter.

Once you send the e-mail, it will arrive in a matter of minutes: no more waiting for the internal mail or post office to deliver your correspondence. And, because of the informality of the medium, your question often will be responded to more quickly as it is appropriate for the receiver to send a reply of only a few words or sentences. The time and effort spent printing and addressing an envelope are also saved. While this may not seem like too much of a time saving, multiply it by five to ten letters a day and the time quickly adds up. (In fact much of this book was written using e-mail messages and a facility that allows users to attach completed documents to messages.)

The accuracy of the system is much higher than that of the post office. If for some reason your mail is undeliverable you will get a message back, within minutes, telling you this: no more waiting weeks for your letter to be returned as undeliverable, and the likelihood of something going astray is decreased.

■ Information storage or production?

Table 7.15 shows that e-mail's basic function is to facilitate communication. Very often the message will not be saved or need to be saved. If the e-mail package has an in-box or filing cabinet component, the software provides an information storage component as well.

Table 7.15 E-mail: information storage or production?

Storage						Production
1	2	3	4	5	6	7

■ Should you use e-mail?

If your colleagues use e-mail, especially on a company network, this is one package worth learning. It will save time and effort, and facilitate the accomplishment of group tasks. Another advantage is that you can easily transfer and receive computer files, such as word processing documents and spreadsheets. If the person you are sending the document to needs to change or re-use the file, he does not need to retype the information.

The first requirement for using this package is that you must have people to whom you can send e-mail. If none of your customers, clients, friends or contacts have e-mail, you will not derive any advantages from using it. However, as more and more people connect to some of the publicly accessible networks and systems described above, there is a greater likelihood that the person you want to mail is connected. As you may be aware, the number of users of the Internet (the global computer system network) is growing by many thousands a month. The situation is similar to the likelihood of dialling a fax machine on your telephone by mistake: a few years ago it was extremely unlikely that you would reach a fax machine, but now it is very likely.

■ Do you really need an e-mail system?

Table 7.16   Do you really need an e-mail system?

	A lot				A little
Time to learn	1	2	3	4	5
Energy to understand	1	2	3	4	5
Learning curve	1	2	3	4	5

Average score _____

■ Products

Lotus *Notes*, *Eudora*, commercial packages such as *CompuServe*, *America On-line*, *Prodigy* and various providers of Internet services.

■ Tracking and storage packages

■ What tracking and storage packages do

Tracking and storage packages essentially help you manage information stored and created with a variety of different programs. One example of this is WordPerfect's *InfoCentral*, which is an object-oriented database. Data are entered and then connected to each other according to the relationships you specify. For instance, you may have *John Smith* listed as a category. Underneath that will be listed different word processing documents, spreadsheets or graphics that are related to this person. Also other documents associated with this person, but not directly about him, can be related to him. If you decide you want to look at a specific document, *InfoCentral* will take you to the application and document, even though you are still in *InfoCentral*. Files can also be retrieved and linked using descriptions, instead of only one word and an extension.

■ Advantages

The main advantage of this, and other tracking and storage packages (see Table 7.17) is that, if you have a difficult time remembering where your documents are, this may assist you. However to have this assistance you have to invest the time to tell the software where each document is.

Table 7.17   Tracking and storage packages: information storage or production?

Storage						Production
1	2	3	4	5	6	7

■ Should you use tracking and storage packages?

If remembering what program your documents are in is difficult, this program may be helpful. If you do not want to spend the time setting this program up, your best strategy is to set up a clear system within each software program to be able to find out where your documents are.

■ Do you really need a tracking and storage program?

Table 7.18   Do you really need a tracking and storage program?

	A lot				A little
Time to learn	1	2	3	4	5
Energy to understand	1	2	3	4	5
Learning curve	1	2	3	4	5

Average score _____

■ Products

WordPerfect *InfoCentral*.

How to choose your software program: summary

Some of the descriptions in the previous sections should help you with choosing software programs from the thousands of software packages that will perform useful functions. Some can be purchased for as little as $50, while others will cost several hundred. It is impossible to use or to understand all of them, so your best strategy is to decide what category of software programs you need, determine what your specific needs are, and then choose your program by asking for recommendations, reading reviews and looking at demonstration programs.

For some types of programs, you may want to go with a package that is a household name. For other types of software programs, you may not have heard any comments and your research and testing of demonstration programs will have to be more detailed. One caveat: in the course of doing your research, you may find hundreds of interesting programs that perform useful tasks. If this task is something that is central to your job, this is a program you should consider using. If, however, it does not relate to your job or your goals, and especially if you are still in the learning stage with computers, save it for a later date. As we have already warned, installing and trying to learn too many software programs at once is a guarantee of failure.

■ Computer hardware devices

Computer systems to deal with electronic information essentially fall into two categories: desktop-based personal computers (PCs) or newer, even more 'personal' computers, one of which is the 'personal digital assistant' (or PDA) such as the Apple *Newton* or the *Psion Organiser*. It is important to realise that these are completely different kinds of computer. Apart from the obvious differences in size (PCs sit on your desk and are not easily portable), there are many differences in the kinds of function you can perform, in the ways you can connect them together and in the basic technology that PCs and PDAs are based on.

It is one of our beliefs that 'more personal' computers, such as PDAs, will eventually replace the desktop computer (as desktop personal computers are gradually replacing the larger and older 'mini-' and 'mainframe' computers). This is due to the incredible pace of technological development in areas such as displays (they are getting smaller, lighter, cheaper, easier to read and of better quality), memory (it is now possible to store megabytes of electronic information on small memory cards which can be carried in the palm of the hand) and in the speed, reliability and size of the processors and other components which are crammed into tiny PDA boxes.

This replacement is not something that will happen in the short term, however. It is therefore worthwhile considering in some detail what devices such as PDAs can do, and whether you can make the move to using them as part of your professional working life. In the next section we will look at PDAs and some other devices which are better classed as computer 'peripherals' – things which are not part of the computer itself but which, when connected, provide extra functions and ways of storing, retrieving and managing information.

■ Personal digital assistants (PDAs)

■ What personal digital assistants (PDAs) do

These devices, the first of which was the Apple *Newton/MessagePad*, were first marketed a long time ago but so far have failed to capture a wide audience. They are very small, hand-held computers, many of which provide 'pen-based input' – the ability to use a pen-like stylus to write directly onto the screen. PDAs offering this also provide 'handwriting recognition', which can translate your handwriting into printed text. Handwriting recognition, however, is still a relatively new development and many users have been disappointed with the results. While many of the devices have a reported 95 per cent accuracy, the 5 per cent that they do not recognise can be quite irritating. Other types of PDAs (such as the Psion *Organiser*) provide an extremely small keyboard (with the full QWERTY key layout as on most PC keyboards). These provide almost the full range of features of a normal computer keyboard, but since they are very small this can result in typing errors, especially when trying to produce long documents. Other features of PDAs include communications facilities (either using infra-red, which allows you to 'beam' messages to another PDA or a PC with the same capability, or using modems to plug the PDA into a conventional telephone line) and enhanced memory facilities (often using very small plug-in cards known as 'PC-cards') which provide additional memory of several megabytes. These are extremely light, portable and resilient, and are convenient for storing information separately (you might have one card for your accounts, another for letters, and so on). PC-cards also provide communications functions, since they can contain the circuitry for small modems to connect to telephone lines, or ones to plug into a cellular telephone. PDAs usually come with personal information software that includes a calendar, to-do list, note taking software and an address book. To perform other operations, software must be purchased, as with a desktop computer.

■ Advantages

The most obvious advantage of PDAs is that they are extremely transportable and lightweight, and allow you to store essential information without the need for a large computer system. For someone who has information to remember, yet whose word processing and other information management needs are not great, this is a useful tool. PDAs are becoming increasingly sophisticated as a result of new technological developments. It is interesting to note that many professionals are starting to use PDAs (often specially adapted) as part of their normal work in areas such as maintenance (where field-workers need to enter and record data when away from the office, for example) or for so-called 'walking workers' (who need to be mobile for some of their time). However the size advantage can often be a disadvantage – they are also easy to lose. We have heard of many experiences of people putting down their PDA in a pile of papers and leaving it behind, or leaving it in another jacket or bag. PDAs are also limited in that, despite the sophisticated circuitry and systems which they use, they are quite heavy consumers of battery power. Being tied to a mains lead when batteries run out defeats the object of having a small, mobile computer. Despite this, many more people are using PDAs and this is stimulating new technical developments in small, faster and cheaper products.

■ Information storage or production?

This is rated a 2 (Table 7.19). The device's main function is to store information, although it is very capable of producing information.

Table 7.19   PDAs: information storage or production?

Storage						Production
1	2	3	4	5	6	7

■ Do you need this?

If you have a job where you are constantly working in the field, the PDA will allow you to take all of your client information and history with you. If you have a personal computer, you may find this device duplicates that machine, although information can be transferred back and forth. Table 7.20 will help you decide whether a PDA is for you.

Table 7.20   Do you really need a PDA?

	A lot				A little
Time to learn	1	2	3	4	5
Energy to understand	1	2	3	4	5
Learning curve	1	2	3	4	5

Average score _____

■ Products

Sharp *Wizard*, Psion *Organiser*, Apple *Newton/MessagePad*, Motorola *Envoy*.

■ CD-Rom

■ What a CD-Rom does?

CD-Rom (*C*ompact *D*isk *R*ead-*O*nly *M*emory) is a computer peripheral that accesses information. To use a CD-Rom you need a CD-Rom 'drive' which reads the CD, and the CD itself. (There are also CDs which can be used to store your own information, but the hardware required is still expensive.) Some of the popular CD programs are encyclopaedias, atlases and telephone directory listings. Other leisure-oriented subjects include books, poetry and recipes. These CDs are distinguished from software packages whose program files may be on a CD-Rom as well as diskettes. Other entertainment-oriented subjects on CDs include a *KGB/CIA World FactBook, Britain at Its Best,* literary works and various cookbooks. Children's games also are one of the more popular CD topics.

■ Advantages

The advantage of having information on a CD-Rom is that a large amount of information can be stored efficiently and retrieved easily. One CD takes up a lot less space then a set of encyclopaedias, or an atlas of the world. With CD-Roms, you can literally have a mountain of information at your fingertips.

■ Information storage or production?

CD-Roms are exclusively for information storage (Table 7.21). While the information can be printed, it will not produce any document other than printing its contents.

Table 7.21   CD-Rom: information storage or production?

Storage						Production
1	2	3	4	5	6	7

■ Should you use a CD-Rom?

If you have a use for reference information, or like the idea of having telephone numbers (either business or residential numbers or the entire country on one disk) this is a very good tool. Also a wide variety of software is available for children, so if you want to help your children become more familiar with computers, as well as having them use educational programs, then this may be a good idea.

   If you are a novice computer user, or are trying to save money when purchasing your computer system, this is one area that you could eliminate. Encyclopaedias, atlases and telephone directories still work in their paper form, and for many people it is still the best way to gain access to that information. Much of this reference information may also be accessed using on-line services.

■ Do you need a CD-Rom?

Table 7.22   Do you need a CD-Rom?

	A lot				*A little*
Time to learn	1	2	3	4	5
Energy to understand	1	2	3	4	5
Learning curve	1	2	3	4	5

Average score _____

■ Computer back-up systems

While consumers will pay large sums of money to purchase car, life, health and property insurance to protect themselves and their families from various problems and calamities, they often balk at spending several hundred pounds to insure their computer data. A computer is a machine. It breaks down when the hard drive crashes, just as a car breaks down. With a car, the solution is easy: the broken part is replaced. One exhaust system is as good as another, and a newer one is definitely better than a used one. With a computer, you also can replace parts, or even buy a new hard drive. However, if you have not backed up your data with a tape back-up or diskettes and your hard drive crashes, you have lost your data. If you do not mind losing your data, then it is not a problem. But if the idea of lost information, or hours spent retyping data does not sound like a very productive way of spending your time, try backing up your data *before* you have a problem. The information stored on your computer is often infinitely more valuable than the computer itself. In Nicholas Negroponte's book *Being Digital*, he tells the story of visiting the headquarters of a US silicon chip manufacturer, and being asked to declare the value of the laptop computer he was carrying. When he said 'two million dollars', the receptionist looked at his old Apple Powerbook in disbelief and suggested 2000 dollars. Negroponte's point is that his information is far more valuable than his old Powerbook (Negroponte, 1995, p.12).

Of course data are not always crucial. One story told to us by a colleague concerned a man who called his computer consultant and said his computer would not start. When he brought his computer over the consultant attempted to restart it and retrieve whatever information could be salvaged from it. However there was nothing that could be done: the hard drive had crashed. At that point the consultant called the client, explained the situation and asked if he had a recent back-up. The client said that he did not, but that it did not matter: 'I needed to clean off my hard drive anyway,' he said.

This attitude is the exception for most people, but points out a further important concept. If you do not need the data, *remove them from your computer*. Too much data on the computer is just as bad as too much paper and old files sitting in your office. Unnecessary data slow down the performance of your computer because it has to hunt through thousands of files, instead of 50 or 60 files to find the file you want. Keeping old data that is no longer needed also causes your hard drive to fill up. If you have to spend several hundred pounds for additional hard disk space, make sure that the purchase is not prompted by a hard disk that is filled up with data you no longer want, or software programs you no longer use.

If you are going to put valuable information on a computer, it is imperative that you have a back-up system in place, preferably a tape back-up. If you have not, you can expect to lose your data at some point during the life of your computer.

■ Scanning devices

■ What scanners do

While the paperless office is a long way from being a reality (for reasons we pointed out earlier) one peripheral device that can help promote the 'paperless office' is a scanner. Scanners range from large, flat-bed scanners that can scan an entire page very quickly (possibly in colour), to monochrome hand-held scanners that are smaller, cost less and must 'swipe' a paper twice to capture the image. Scanners, with the appropriate software, can capture both text and pictures. Sophisticated scanners are also being used by large companies that are developing and using databases which contain large numbers of digital documents (for example, legal documents) for 'electronic document delivery' (EDD).

■ Advantages

There are many advantages to scanning information into the computer. If you need to refer to and re-use the scanned information in other documents, the retrieval can be easier as you can use key words to search for the data you want. The data can be found within seconds, as opposed to searching in a filing cabinet for 10 or 15 minutes. This is especially true if it is something that you have not referred to lately.

In addition to finding information more quickly, scanning information also gives people in other offices of your company access to it. Instead of your having to fax something to them (at about a minute per page) they can retrieve information from the computer network without having to involve someone else in their efforts.

If your work involves travelling, your scanned documents could easily be retrieved using a computer notebook and connecting into your company's network. Scanned documents also reduce floor-based storage space and provide a neater appearance for offices by eliminating rows of file cabinets and piles of paper.

■ Information storage or production?

A scanner is an information storage tool, which is why it is rated a 1 in Table 7.23. While the information can be taken from the scanner and imported into other packages, the primary function of the scanner is to store information.

Table 7.23   Scanners: information storage or production?

Storage						Production
1	2	3	4	5	6	7

■ Should you use a scanner?

Scanning, while it is a useful facility, is not appropriate for everyone. Scanned documents should be documents that will be referred to again. If they will not be referred to again, the time to scan, and the disk storage space that is used, will not be productive. Scanned documents also occupy much more disk space then the same document does in the word processor. This is because a graphic image is being stored, which occupies more disk space than a regular word processing document. Scanning also takes a lot of time, especially for the initial operation when all the information must be scanned. Make sure the material scanned justifies the time investment. Also, if your information is scanned into the computer, it is crucial that your computer is backed up daily, otherwise your important data may be lost.

■ Do you really need a scanner?

Table 7.24   Do you really need a scanner?

	A lot				A little
Time to learn	1	2	3	4	5
Energy to understand	1	2	3	4	5
Learning curve	1	2	3	4	5

Average score _____

■ Telecommunications

It is important to remember that information is also transmitted or stored in telecommunication devices which must be considered in the same way as the computer-based products we have looked at in this chapter. Here we will look briefly at the major telecommunications devices that can be used in managing information, and which should be included in your PIM strategy. It is important to remember that, just because information is not written down (electronically or on paper), this does not mean that it is not information you need to manage. Managing communications services can prove valuable in streamlining and re-engineering your information management.

■ Pagers

Pagers provide other people with immediate access to you. They allow you to leave your office and be reached quickly in cases of urgency. Most pagers only transmit signals within a 75 mile radius (but some paging services in the USA and UK will work nation-wide). In order to maximise your time, define who should have access to your pager number. If you have an assistant, he or she can perhaps control access to you through your pager.

■ Voice mail

Voice mail, if it is used correctly, can be a wonderful time-saver. Very often all we need is to say a few brief words to a colleague, or to answer his or her specific question. If lengthy messages need to be left with a colleague, voice mail is much more efficient than leaving it with a secretary, where you are not able to see what is actually being written down. The other advantage of voice mail is the ability to respond to inquiries after several hours. As long as people pay prompt attention to their voice mail, it is a wonderful time-saving tool.

■ Cellular telephones

Cellular telephones are another tool that makes it easy to be away from the office. One technique to control costs, and also to maximise your time, is to strictly control or not give out your cellular telephone numbers. Instead, let people use your voice mail or pager. Then you can call them back using the cellular telephone.

■ Sophisticated office telephones

These can save time and effort as they allow routing of one voice message to a number of people who have the same system. This is a very efficient way to remind colleagues on the same voice mail system about a meeting. Conference calling, redial, memorised numbers and a speaker telephone are some of the other features that make these a valuable tool, and one that is capable of saving time and producing efficiencies.

■ Fax

Fax devices are very popular and enjoy widespread use. Computer fax/modems allow you to fax word-processed documents directly from your computer to the recipient's fax machine, saving you the time of printing, walking to the fax machine and making sure the fax goes through. They also eliminate the paper copy of the fax which, more often then not, would end up lying around.

■ Why are computers so difficult to use?

We have spent some time reviewing some of the software and hardware products which are available to help manage personal information. You must now make a decision about which software and hardware products you want to use. At this point, many people see the value of using different software programs, but they hesitate to use a computer because they believe computers are too difficult to use. Understanding a little of the history of the development of office equipment will show the timid user that the problem is not due to stupidity or slowness. Rather he or she is caught up in a generational issue that will not exist for the children who are learning about and using computers in school today.

Until two decades ago, the primary office machine, the typewriter, remained essentially the same in its function as it did when it was invented in 1874 by Remington, the gun manufacturer. While the product was improved over the years and became electric (and then electronic), the user noticed very little difference in the way the typewriter was used. Typewriters served a production function, creating letters and documents. The paper which the letter was typed on provided the information storage function, and the paper was stored separately from the typewriter. It has only been in the last 15 years or so that the level of complexity increased with the introduction of electronic typewriters. These new typewriters could now store information, such as form letters, and had a screen where you could see what you typed before it was printed. A typist using an early 1900s typewriter could switch to a 1950s version with minor difficulty. A switch to an electronic typewriter could also be made relatively easily. The electronic machine could be mastered within several hours.

Now imagine switching from a 1950s typewriter to a personal computer. While the computer can do much more than the typewriter, its complexity also has increased dramatically. Indeed the computer today is about as similar to a typewriter as is a forklift truck. And the new computer user has had about as much familiarity and training with the computer as he has with a forklift. There is an entire research field known as 'human–computer interaction' (HCI) that is devoted to understanding the problems people have with computers and trying to develop solutions.

The computer and typewriter look the same as they have the same key layout, and this has remained the same since the first typewriter device was designed (by William Austin Burt) in the 1820s. This device was a box made almost entirely of wood with type mounted on a metal wheel which the user operated by turning a small wheel until the particular letter appeared, and then pulling a lever to imprint the letter on paper. Devices such as these were large, unusable and could not really speed up the process of writing beyond the 30 words per minute which was possible with the fastest writers using pens. The first development towards the modern typewriter was that by the inventors Sholes, Gidden and Soule in the 1860s. The problem with their typewriter, however, was that users could hit each key too quickly and as a result the keys jammed as the typist's speed increased. As a result Sholes redesigned the keyboard of the typewriter to slow the typist down, which produced the now universally familiar QWERTY key layout (named after the left-hand top row keys). Although the new design certainly removed the key-jamming problem, it was not maximally convenient for typists since, to achieve any speed with the keyboard, users were forced to move away from the two-finger 'hunt and peck' style of typing to a method of typing using all the fingers. The 'touch method', as it came to be known, is attributed to Frank E. McGurrin, who taught himself how to use all of his fingers while not looking at the keyboard and so increased his typing speed. The development of other 'touch methods' provided the basis for touch-typing contests in the 1880s and increased the sales of typewriters produced by manufacturers such as Remington. As a result, between 1905 and 1915, over 100 different typewriter manufacturers appeared and by 1898 there were some 60 000 female typists in the USA, trained in many newly established typewriting schools.

This history of the typewriter is also the history of the modern keyboard attached to the computer. Unfortunately the QWERTY key layout has been a source of considerable problems because of the need to learn a touch-typing method and because of the difficulties caused by the uncomfortable postures that users have to adopt when using the keyboard. And, since the problems of key-jamming are of course eliminated in the computer, there is no real reason why the computer keyboard should be laid out in the QWERTY design.

An entire generation of people have been presented with personal computers and told to use them so they can be 'more efficient'. However in many cases they have had only a few hours in a training class or, worse, no training at all. In addition to learning the computer, they still had to perform their job functions. Many people did not even know how to operate a typewriter. Contrast this training situation with learning to type. To learn how to use the typewriter, students took a year-long typing class in high school. This was a time when they could gradually learn to use the typewriter and were under no pressure to produce actual work. School assignments were designed to meet their skill level. Even if someone did not get any more experience typing than from a class, he could use a typewriter to type a letter or a form without too much trouble, even though he would naturally be slow. For the person (probably a woman) who was interested in working in an office, she might attend business school for additional training. Then her job became helping her boss get his work done: managing information (filing) and producing documents (typing). She was trained for her job and her boss, who had no training in this area, did not even have to attempt to be knowledgeable.

Beginning in the 1980s, as corporations began to 'downsize', and as personal computers began to appear in offices, it was expected that managers would use computers and so reduce the need for secretarial support. Now the professional who previously was never expected to type letters was given a computer, told to start using it and had to begin learning. It did not matter that he had never encountered anything like this before. True, he may have attended a training class, but at best it lasted only one day – a difference from the year-long typing class. And a typewriter is much less complex than a computer. Is it any wonder people are experiencing a great deal of frustration?

In fact, there is no other machine as complex and that we attempt to learn with so little training or time commitment. When we learn to drive a car (depending on what country we are in), we may take 25–50-hours of driving lessons. After the basics are learned, we begin to drive with an instructor. Once this is accomplished, the driver can get a learner's permit that allows him to drive with a licensed driver, and then, finally, a permanent licence. Contrast this with what happens with a new computer: once it is out of the box, you are expected to 'drive' the computer by yourself straightaway. Maybe the answer is licensed computer users!

Don Norman, in his book, *Things That Make Us Smart*, offers one explanation for computers being so difficult to learn. He states that there does not have to be any natural relationship between the *appearance* of the object and its *state*. For instance, when a paper file is stuffed with information, it is very visible. If we remember that the file is very thick (and a particular colour), that will help us to retrieve the file. If an electronic file folder is stuffed with information, the perception of the file's contents is totally dependent upon whoever designed it. Typically the person designing the software is very comfortable and familiar with computers; the person using the computer is likely to be much less comfortable with them (Norman, 1993, p.79).

For example, a common computer command in the MSDOS operating system, which has existed throughout the various versions, is the 'Make a Directory' command. (A directory is equivalent to a drawer of a filing cabinet. It contains similar information, or all of the program files needed to run one software program. The directory keeps all of this information together in the computer.) What might be easier for the new computer user would be the terminology to 'make a filing drawer' or 'create a filing drawer', as everyone inherently understands a filing cabinet and probably has used one. However the command for the computer is 'make directory' – but you do not use those words. Instead you must type MD (or, on the UNIX operating system, mkdir). To the computer programmer this is perfectly clear. To almost everyone else, this is just one of the little quirks that produces complexity and makes computers frustrating.

■ How to make using a computer easier

Although better and better software and operating systems (such as Microsoft *Windows* and the Apple *Macintosh*) are being designed, often with the help of users, to ensure that they are flexible, intuitive, easy to use and simple to learn, there is still a long way to go before computers are completely intuitive. For the moment, it is easy to see that, as people experience problems with computers, they often respond in two ways. One way is to get frustrated and angry, the other is to fear and loathe computers. Neither response, while understandable, really helps with the goal of working efficiently or managing information effectively.

If someone wants to make the transition to a computer, the following will help make their transition as easy as possible.

■ You can learn how to use the computer

If you *believe* you can learn how to use the computer and software programs, it is certain you will learn. If, however, you believe that the computer is too hard to use, or you despise it, you can assume that you will never learn it. Perhaps the best way is to take a gradual approach to learning the system. Also do not put yourself in a position of *immediately* having to produce a final copy with your new-found computer skills. Give yourself a chance to absorb what you have learned and congratulate yourself on what you have accomplished. Do not criticise yourself for what you did not understand.

■ Establish a plan for learning to use the computer

Establish an action plan for learning a new software program or a new computer. There are several ways to approach learning a new software package. For someone who has the 'do-it-yourself approach', he or she can block off an hour or two to install the software and begin learning to use it. The key to learning the program is not to try to do it all at once. Remember, learning software and a computer system is like learning to drive. You do not expect to take a cross-country trip after your first driving lesson. Do not expect to become an expert computer user in a few hours.

Once the initial stage is complete, the user can approach the situation in one of two ways. He can begin to use the program, either typing in data or beginning to do some basic work. The other approach, for someone who is more nervous, is to schedule four to six half-hour sessions to learn how to use the program, without any expectation of producing a final product. Whichever option is chosen, it is important to try not to expect to accomplish too much too quickly. Remember, you are not yet an experienced user and should not expect to produce work like one. Take the process slow and easy and learn along the way. Soon you will be an experienced user.

As you are learning a software program, use the 'help' feature extensively.

Many products have a search feature so you can type in the subject you have a question about. When you are given that information, it will briefly explain that feature, and show you the steps for accessing it. This is a quick way to learn how to accomplish a specific task, and it avoids dealing with a large book and hunting for what you need.

The opposite of the do-it-yourself approach is the 'do-it-for-me' approach. For someone short on time or patience, this is a viable alternative. Hiring a consultant to set up a computer system or to install a software program is a quick and easy way to get the job accomplished. What consultants cannot do is transfer *their* knowledge of the computer into *your* brain. Unfortunately that process must rely on old-fashioned methods such as practice. In order to help short-circuit the learning process, there are several things that can be done. For one thing, once the consultant has finished installing and setting up the software, pay him or her to stay for an additional hour and thoroughly explain the product and its frequently used functions. If you remember information by taking notes, be sure to do that. Ask plenty of questions. One lesson may not be enough: if your time is valuable and limited, several one-hour lessons with the consultant to answer questions and show you other features may be warranted.

Another way to help short-circuit the learning process is to attend a class or buy a training video for beginners. Also use any tutorial programs that come with your software program.

■ Purchase software from the same company

Purchasing software products from one company helps reduce the steepness of your learning curve. Some of the major software companies now have 'office suites' of applications. These are several programs that perform different office functions such as word processing, spreadsheets and databases. The advantage of using all of the products from one company is that many of the commands will be similar. You can expect the programs within one suite to have very similar commands for common features such as *print*, *save*, *copy* and *spell check*. A command learned for one program will work in another. Learning one program facilitates the learning of the second program. Also, because the same company makes the programs, information can be swapped relatively easily between the programs.

■ Other computer issues

■ How quickly should you upgrade?

It never fails. Just as soon as you become familiar with your favourite software program, a new version appears. What do you do? Do you upgrade immediately? Or do you wait around until the following upgrade is out and you are facing obsolescence?

That all depends. Do you have problems with the product? Does it seem like it has bugs in it? Do you need the program to do more things? If the answer to any of these questions is 'yes', you should upgrade as quickly as possible. Install the upgrade when you do not have the pressure of an immediate deadline. While it is the same product, new features will make it different from the old one and will require some learning time. You can expect the learning curve with an upgrade to be less steep than it would be with a new software package.

If you upgrade, the program should automatically transform your data into a format compatible with the previous version. You will not have to re-enter any data or lose anything as a result of the upgrade.

■ Must you upgrade?

The answer is 'yes' – at some point you must. Computer technology moves ahead, and refusing to move forward with it means that eventually you will soon have to learn and purchase a new system, exactly as if you had never used a computer before. And as new software and upgrades are introduced they will increasingly require new and more powerful hardware. However you do not need to be the first person on the block to have the latest and greatest version. If you do not want to trouble-shoot computer problems, it makes sense to wait until the new products and upgrades have been out a while and the company has had a chance fix some of the problems that were not solved in the development stage.

■ Continuous learning

No matter how much you try to learn about computers, your knowledge will not last forever. New products will be developed, and the ones you liked so well will become obsolete. To use computers effectively, you must continue learning, whether it is learning a new version of a software program or understanding your current software program better. One way to improve your knowledge is, each time you begin to use a software package, to learn one new feature. This does not need to take more than a few minutes.

Unlike the typewriter that was mastered soon after typing class was over, the computer requires continual learning.

CHAPTER 8

Paper-based information products

While we have so far discussed technological tools for managing information, most people still use paper as the primary medium for storing and producing information. When people decide to organise their office, paper is usually the primary motivating item and many of the items in our office (desk, cabinets, trays and shelves) are there to support our extensive use of paper, even though we may have a sophisticated computer network available. In this chapter will discuss, and offer some hints on managing, paper-based information.

■ Categories of paper-based information

Paper appears in many different forms in the office. Some papers are categorised into files, others are randomly placed around the office. Paper-based information is also contained in Post-it notes, wall calendars, daily 'to-do' lists, personal organisers, books and magazines.

There are five general reasons to keep information, as outlined by Katherine Aschner in *Taking Control of Your Office Records: A Manager's Guide* (Aschner, 1983):

1. *Operating requirements*: these will include such things as client information, correspondence or other records that support the functioning of your job or business.
2. *Administrative requirements*: often these files provide support after the operating requirements have been meet. They may involve a summary of the past month's activity. Within this category may also be 'personal' administrative files such as company memos or policies, as well as correspondence or expense account information.
3. *Fiscal requirements*: these are financial documents, including sales, accounts receivable and income tax information.
4. *Legal requirements*: these are any records or documents needed in the case of disputes or litigation. They may be client documents in disputes over the work performed, or financial records such as payments and invoices in the case of non-payment.
5. *Historical requirements*: these are papers that in the future will have a great historical significance. They may include such things as an invoice that signifies the $1 million point in sales. However Aschner cautions that these represent only about 5 per cent of all documents (Aschner, 1983, pp.39–40).

For corporate employees, their personal information will fall mainly into the *operating*, *administrative* or *fiscal* categories. Small business owners will have information in all five of the categories.

■ Operating requirements

The following kinds of information are typically found in offices. They can be expected to fall under one of these categories.

■ Current projects/areas of responsibility

For each project or area of responsibility, you will need to use and save relevant reports, letters and memos. For each area, the papers should be stored in their own file. These files may be broken down into more detail, or each subject area may require more than one file. For example, if one of your responsibilities is marketing, you may have a marketing file. Inside you may have sub-files pertaining to business cards, brochures and television advertising. Or, if the information is particularly voluminous, each sub-file may be in a file by itself.

■ Client files

The same situation exists with client files. Each client should have their own file or files. Sub-categories can be created according to particular issues. Sub-files also can be created for correspondence, clients' documents or billing.

■ Magazines

This is one category of information that people love to save, but the value of the information decreases rapidly. Some of the clients we have helped have insisted that the information contained in the magazines is very important and must be saved. This is said even though we point out that one magazine, several months or years old, is still in its plastic wrapping. Information is worthless unless it is read and absorbed. It can not be absorbed through a plastic wrapper.

□ Tips for managing

If you can not make time to read the entire magazine (most people can not) then try this strategy. Designate your commuting time, or another time period, as time to scan the table of contents, pick out the one or two articles that have the most relevance for you, read those two, and then discard the magazine. Yes, you *should* read the entire magazine, but let us face the truth. When are you going to have time to do that? If you want to save the article, pull it out of the magazine and file it with the client or project area that it relates to the most. It is not good enough to save the article and then never refer to it again. Instead, put it where you will find it. Do not store old magazines and journals. Usually their only purpose is to consume shelf space. Instead, if you read an important article you want to keep, clip it and then file it appropriately. Discontinue magazine subscriptions if you continue not to have time to read them. Anything that is not urgent enough for you to make the time to read it, is probably not critical. For most publications you can purchase the magazine on the news-stand when you have time to read it.

■ Books

Books, by their nature, are created for long-term information storage and reference. A well-made book will last many years. However, just because a book lasts a long time, this does not mean it has to belong to you. If you are running out of storage room for your books, go through them carefully and see which are no longer relevant to your current work. On careful examination you will be surprised how many books you no longer need or want. Often we buy books that teach us concepts or give us information. Once we have learned that information, we do not necessarily need the book. Share the knowledge you gained from the book by donating it to a library sale or charity or passing it on to a friend.

□ Tips for managing

Go through your books once a year and determine which are no longer relevant to your profession and personal situation. If you have not opened a book in the last two years, it is likely that you do not need it and it can be safely donated, especially if you are short of space.

■ Newspapers

Most people tend to read one newspaper a day, in addition to listening to television or radio news. While newspapers are valuable, this is one reading item that can be eliminated for the busy professional who insists that he does not have enough hours in the day.

□ Tips for managing

Instead of spending a half-hour reading a newspaper during commuting or before work time, spend that time reading a professional journal, mail or reports that you have not been able to make time for during the previous day. When you are not as pressed for time, you can always purchase a newspaper at a news-stand. Cancel your subscription and buy a copy on the mornings that you do have time to read it.

■ Business cards

One thing that always seems to collect in pockets, briefcases and on desk tops are business cards. The card's importance depends on whether this is the card of a client or one of someone you met the previous night at a business function and are only mildly interested in contacting again.

□ Tips for managing

Instead of lying around, the card should immediately go into a Rolodex or computer database, depending on whichever system you choose. If you want to do a follow-up letter, do that the following day. Nothing loses its information value more quickly than a business card that has lain around for several weeks or months without being filed and without having any information attached to, it such as where the person was met and what was discussed.

■ Future projects

Sometimes information is collected for projects that are anticipated. For instance, if you are planning to purchase a new computer, you may save advertisements and articles about computers. Or, if you have a corporate event to plan, you may save relevant information long before the due date. Each of these items should have its own file.

□ Tips for managing

While this is a good way to begin planning for a project, when it is complete you can probably discard the file. If you need reference materials for the next similar event, go through the file and discard the information that is not essential. This saves storage space and time spent searching through irrelevant information.

■ Post-it notes/to-do lists

Post-it notes have grown in value since they were 'accidentally' developed by the 3M Corporation. They are excellent for jotting notes on documents. Neon-coloured Post-its add an extra dimension. However, carried to an extreme, Post-it notes can become a problem. Often they are used to make to-do lists. Some people figure that if one to-do list is a good thing, then ten are better. Each time they think of something that should be done, they write it on a Post-it note. Each new idea goes on another piece of paper. Soon managing the papers becomes a project in itself. While Post-it notes can be useful as a quick reminder of something that needs to be done immediately, be cautious about using them too often, or as your only system.

□ Tips for managing

While putting a bright note next to your phone to remind you to call someone is not a bad idea, if it is your only system then it probably can be improved. If you want to prompt yourself to remember different items using individual notes, at the very least group them or stick them onto a folder or a clipboard so you can see at a glance what needs to be done. Otherwise first on your list will be finding the notes that tell you what needs to be done.

■ Wall calendars

These devices are wonderful for planning purposes or for outlining deadlines for group or long-term projects. What they are not good at doing is providing a method for writing in your daily appointments.

□ Tips for managing

Use wall calendars for tracking group projects or to outline the stages in a long-term project. Clever graphics can tell staff members instantly whether the project is behind schedule or ahead of schedule.

■ Paper-based personal organisers

While numerous software versions of popular, paper-based personal organisers have been introduced in recent years, many people are still clinging to their paper-based system, and for good reasons. The advantage of the paper-based system is that you do not need to learn how to use paper, other than understanding a few key concepts. The other advantage is that, the system is extremely portable. The disadvantage of the paper-based system is that, if the information is to be used to produce a client list, or as part of a mailing, it must be entered into the computer. If any of the information changes, it then must be changed twice.

□ Tips for managing

If you are away from your computer for long time periods, it is probably a good thing to keep your schedule and your to-do list with you so you can check your availability if you need to arrange meetings or let people know when you can get requested information to them. If you already have many of your client or contact records on the computer, print out the information from that software program and include it in your personal organiser. Do not handwrite this information in the back of your book, especially if it can be accessed from a printout. The entire point is to save time, not to create more work for you.

■ Personal calendars

While calendars are much simpler devices than personal organisers, they are still very useful. Calendars can be used solely to write appointment times down, not to-do lists, and they can be pocket-sized for maximum portability. Sometimes the simplest tools are the best tools.

■ Administrative requirements

■ Associations

Often professionals belong to networking or non-profit associations. If you have leadership roles, the amount of paper that tends to collect for these functions increases as you will want to keep all minutes and meeting agendas, as well as other supporting materials. Many people get into trouble with this information by still having it years later, even after they no longer have a leadership position, or even after they have dropped their membership. If you are just a member of the group, other than a few introductory pieces of information and a phone listing, the newsletter will be the big item that you receive. This is something that you do not need to keep, beyond the time period that it addresses. However this is an example of the kind of papers that people tend to save. The result is that the important papers end up getting tangled up with these storage papers. Instead of providing any value, they create confusion.

□ Tips for managing

If you must keep this information, keep no more than one year's worth. If this tip has you going through withdrawal, you can keep two years' information (but no more). Professional associations often have offices or storage areas. Let the storage function be performed there, not in your office. With association newsletters, read them in five minutes, capture the main news, put the next meeting on your calendar, then throw them away. These documents lose value very quickly after the time period has passed. What useful purpose does it serve to have information about a meeting or a job opening that is six months old?

■ Unread mail

The next category of information that loses its value very quickly is unread mail. Almost everyone can be counted upon to look at their mail and pick out the important documents. What they often do, however, is set aside the mail that is not deemed important, to be looked at 'later on'. Unfortunately 'later on' never arrives. Instead unread mail piles up, and eventually a problem builds up.

☐ Tips for managing

Look at all of your mail as it comes in. Do not save it for looking at later. If it does not prompt you to do something with it immediately, you can be guaranteed that it will not increase in value several weeks or months down the road. Basically decisions can be made in ten seconds or less about what should be done with unsolicited mail.

■ Company memos

While some company information has important, long-term value, most of it does not. Instead many of the memos deal with subjects such as the time and place of the Christmas party – the one that was six months ago. Keeping this information often hinders the retrieval of the information that is important, and uses up valuable storage space, which can be put to better use.

☐ Tips for managing

Memos and other company information, such as newsletters, should be read when they are received and the information absorbed or inserted in your calendar as necessary. Then they can be discarded soon after the issue or event has occurred. If a document has information that is of lasting value, that should be retained.

■ Fiscal requirements

Very often people have responsibility for their company's budget or expenditures. Relevant information should stay in its own file.

■ Legal requirements

With luck this category is not one that you deal with or need. However you may need to save information for legal requirements, either in anticipation of a lawsuit or after a lawsuit has been concluded.

■ Historical requirements

This is an area that most people will not be concerned about. Instead someone in a specific role in a company is likely to be assigned the task of maintaining the archives. However you may want to save items that would be appropriate to your accomplishments. Be cautious about what you do retain. This is a category that can get quickly out of control when too many things are deemed to have a historical value.

CHAPTER 9

Your personal information management strategy

The previous chapters have, it is hoped, provided you with a great deal of useful, and new, information about the problems of information overload and about personal information management, and have given you some analyses of, and some suggestions about, various types of personal information management technologies. Table 9.1 lists the information storage tools we have discussed. Now that you have a basic understanding of what they can do, you have a basis for choosing the tools you need. You can now combine that knowledge with the knowledge of what information you need, according to your goals.

This book does not intend to give recommendations for specific brands of products. In order to decide which brands you would like to purchase, take the following steps:

- ask business acquaintances and friends for recommendations;
- look for product reviews via on-line services, computer bulletin boards or computer magazines;
- seek out demonstration disks where the product can be used and tested for its suitability.

After doing these three things, you will be in a good position to choose the product that will work best for you. To start the process of developing your own PIM strategy, which we will discuss in detail in the next chapter, complete Table 9.1. In conducting this exercise, you may find that the software package you wanted to use, or are using, is not as helpful as it could be. Using the information in paper form may even be a better solution. Similarly you may find that it would make more sense to have your paper-based information in a software package.

Remember, whether you use paper or technology to help you manage information, they are still tools and only a means to an end, not the end in themselves. Make certain that the tools you use fit your purpose.

Table 9.1 PIM strategy development chart

Technology	Yes	No	Product	Keep for how long?
Software				
Spreadsheets				
Databases				
Word processors				
Personal organisers				
Calendars				
E-mail				
Computer hardware				
Personal digital assistants				
CD-Rom				
Scanners				
Computer networks				
Internet				
CompuServe				
Delphi				
Telecommunications				
Pagers				
Fax				
Voice mail				
Cellphones				
Office phones				
Paper				
Files				
Post-it notes				
Wall calendars				
To-do lists				
Books				
Magazines				
Time management systems				
Calendars				

Producing and implementing your own personal information management strategy

It's easy enough to be a starter, but are you a sticker too? It's easy enough to begin a job. It's harder to see it through. (Margaret Thatcher)

This is a very apt quotation to describe the challenge of implementing your PIM strategy. While you may have developed a good theory of what your strategy should look like, unless it is implemented its value is negligible. This implementation, unfortunately, involves seemingly time-consuming and tedious things such as going through existing papers, deciding which ones are important and should be kept, where they should be put and which ones should be discarded. We use the word 'unfortunately' because, for every client we have worked with, this process was the one they liked the least. More than once a client of ours has stated, 'If you weren't here helping, I would have quit a few hours ago.' But the good news is that, after the initial aversion to going through their archives, some people begin to get excited about the progress they are making: a desk that they can now see and the number of bin liners that are being filled.

You should have a good idea of what tools you want to use to manage information. You may also have some idea of information that really is not important and can be eliminated. The point of a PIM strategy is to create a situation where you can retrieve any information you need, when you need it, and spend only seconds doing so. While time management has been one of the key business improvement or self-improvement strategies of the 1980s, the value of time management greatly diminishes if you have to spend an unscheduled 20 to 45 minutes a day searching for papers or computer files. While 45 minutes a day may seem excessive, many of our clients say that it is common for them to spend that long. This is why time management alone does not help. Instead, you must combine good time management techniques with a clear vision of what you need to do and the knowledge and ability to find the information you need. You must create your own PIM strategy.

While time management techniques have much value in many instances, some ideas must be approached with caution. In her book, *Surviving Information Overload* (1992), Kathryn Alesandrini lists several 'time management myths'. One of these is '*never handle a piece of paper more than once*'. While handling a piece of paper only once may sound like a good suggestion, the reality is that many pieces of paper must be handled many times. Would you want to handle the draft for a crucial proposal only once, or would you want to handle it many times, double checking your ideas and presentation and sharing it with other team members? From our experience of working with paper (and with electronic documents such as this book, which was stored solely in electronic form, not on paper) important documents need to be handled *many* times, whether in electronic or paper form. Simple documents (memos, letters, circulars) may be amenable to the 'only handle it once' rule, but for many of us, dealing with important projects and the information associated with them, this is not adequate.

Another idea Alesandrini calls a 'myth' is to '*carefully plan ahead and schedule your time on a daily basis*'. Too much scheduling can eliminate impromptu calls or visits from co-workers that may be important. One of the key concepts of business success today is *flexibility* and too rigid a schedule will eliminate the possibility of being flexible.

■ Your PIM strategy is derived from your goals

Your PIM strategy is developed from your personal and business goals. Any information necessary to help you fulfil your goals is important and should be included in your strategy. A PIM strategy provides a structure for you to make decisions about what information is important and what is not. Without that distinction, any information will seem relevant, and the probability of retaining too much information, especially information that will never be referred to again, is great. The problem that occurs with retaining too much information, as we have seen, is information overload, which means that, when you do need something that you have not seen for a long time, you have just that many more other pieces of (irrelevant) information to search through to find the information you need.

The necessity of having a PIM strategy is summed up by an episode from Lewis Carroll's *Alice in Wonderland* (1984, pp.89–90). Alice asks the Cheshire Cat:

'Would you tell me, please, which way I ought to walk from here?'
'That depends a good deal on where you want to get to' said the Cat.
'I don't much care where' said Alice.
'Then it doesn't matter which way you walk' said the Cat.
'So long as I get somewhere' Alice added as an explanation.
'Oh, you're sure to do that' said the Cat, 'if you only walk long enough.'

It is the same with your PIM strategy. If you do not know what your goals are, or what the accompanying important information is, then it really does not matter what information you save and what you eliminate. The first step in developing your strategy is to know what information is important to you.

■ Information is perishable

While a PIM strategy can sound dauntingly complex, in fact it is very simple to create. If you have bought groceries and put them away, whether a few items from the store after work or a full week's shopping, you are capable of creating and maintaining a PIM strategy. Here is how these two tasks are similar. A PIM strategy involves *knowing what information you want, knowing where it should be* and *putting it there*. Grocery shopping involves the same steps. You must know what food you need to buy. Then you must know where the food should go, once you have it at home, and then it must be put in its proper place.

We use this analogy because, first, nearly everyone has at some point in their life gone shopping for groceries. And second, in *all* of our experience working with clients who want to organise their office (or home office), groceries are the one item that are never a problem. Groceries were always put in their proper place as soon as they were brought into the office or house. Canned goods are placed on the appropriate shelf with the other canned goods. Fresh fruit goes in the appropriate drawer in the refrigerator. Laundry detergent goes on a utility room shelf. Toothpaste, shampoos and soaps go in the bathroom. Frozen foods are placed immediately in the freezer, otherwise they will be ruined. Milk, cheese and meat go straight into the refrigerator, otherwise they will spoil and have to be thrown out. If they are thrown out, the money, time and effort it took to purchase them will also have been wasted. The entire operation is accomplished in five minutes or less.

A fact that many people do not realise is that information 'spoils' just as readily as fresh food. An important memo or article that you want to use for a client project, if it is lying at the bottom of your desk, or randomly stuck in a filing cabinet, will be of no use if you do not know it exists or cannot find it. Coming across it a month later, after the project is completed, is a good example of the way important information is spoilt. While people will state that all of their pieces of paper are very important, they often do not take care of them very well. This is equivalent to leaving a frozen pizza out all day. It may be very important for tomorrow night's dinner but it is not going to be worth anything if it is not put in its correct place – the freezer.

■ The importance of information decreases with time

Information has a unique property. As time passes its importance decreases (see Figure 9.1). For example, do you remember a letter that sparked a huge argument and battle within your company? Everyone was running for cover and hastily justifying their actions in the matter. Now that same letter, six months later, is old news. What was so crucial then has been forgotten and passed over. This is why it is good to review your information thoroughly once every six months to a year. Issues, ideas and priorities change and it is no use having the remnants of a discarded project left around.

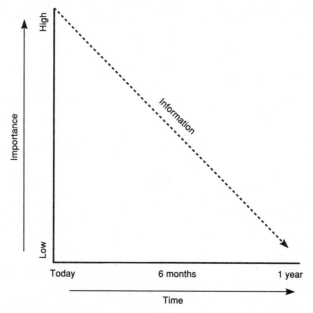

Figure 9.1 The importance of information

Yet, while many people acknowledge the decreasing importance of information, they are often reluctant to change their habits. Instead important information is retained, even though it is buried in the corners of an office, or under newer papers at the top of a sideboard or desk. And if it was actually needed, finding it would be a major stroke of luck. So the next question is, if you are not going to be able to find information, or have to spend a great deal of time looking for it, why should you hang onto it in the first place? A PIM strategy helps you stop important information from 'spoiling' by giving you the correct place to put. Filing a piece of paper in the correct spot takes no more time than putting the milk in the refrigerator.

■ Benefits of a PIM strategy

We talked earlier in general terms about the benefits of 're-engineering' your information management. We will now look at some of those benefits in detail, along with some of the reasons many people say they do not 'need to' or 'don't want to' 're-engineer'. There are four primary benefits of creating your own PIM strategy: stress reduction, a decrease in feelings of 'being overwhelmed', time saving and increased efficiency.

■ Stress

Stress is reduced by eliminating the fear of not being able to find the information you need when you need it. For anyone working without the benefit of a PIM strategy, the thought of having to find specific information immediately produces a nagging fear of not being able to do so. Then the fear turns into irritation and self-criticism when they actually cannot find the needed information. This in turn creates stress.

■ Being overwhelmed

Feelings of being overwhelmed can be decreased by getting organised. Often clients look at their desk and see the mountains of 'work' that needs to be done. Telephone messages, files and mail all look as if they will take a week or longer to handle. However, after sorting through their papers to implement their PIM strategy, they often find that the work they thought needed to be done is now irrelevant. Putting their PIM strategy into place ensures that their feeling of being overwhelmed decreases as their pile of papers decreases.

■ Time saving

A PIM strategy saves time because you are no longer looking for information. Take a moment to consider how much time during the average day you spend looking for information. Is it five minutes, 15 minutes or 45 minutes? While at first the time does not seem too important, consider how quickly it adds up. Fifteen minutes a day, over a year equals 65 hours. This is equivalent to a one and a half weeks' holiday. Often the same people who spend 15 minutes a day searching for lost information say they are 'too busy' to take a day off or have a holiday. Take a minute to do your own calculation. How much time do you spend each day looking for information or worrying that you cannot find something?

■ Efficiency

Working more efficiently is also a benefit. Instead of dispersing your efforts, you must focus your attention on the most important things to be done. If you have only two hours available to produce an important report, how much time do you want to spend gathering and finding your materials? Do you really want to spend the first half-hour just trying to get organised and locate your information? Having a PIM strategy allows you to work efficiently by eliminating time wasted looking for information. Instead you can focus on the important task in hand.

■ Benefits quiz

To get an idea of how you might benefit from a PIM strategy, try the questionnaire (Table 9.2).

□ Results

51–70 points   This score indicates that a PIM strategy carefully thought out and implemented would be very beneficial to you.
25–50 points   While your score could be better, you are doing an average job of managing your information. You can achieve major efficiencies by implementing a PIM strategy.
8–24 points   You are doing a very good job of managing your information. Take a look at the questions where you scored highest and use your PIM strategy to improve those areas.

■ Roadblocks to effective personal information management

While many people will state their desire to become better organised, often they come up with 'roadblocks' along the way to prevent them from achieving that goal. Some issues, such as an increased workload, or a busy period, are of course beyond personal control. Other factors, such as procrastination or feelings of being overwhelmed, are difficult to cope with, but they are definitely under our

Table 9.2 PIM strategy benefits questionnaire

Benefits questionnaire Circle your answer to the following questions. At the end, add up your score.

How often do you feel stressed by not being able to find information you urgently need?

Never	Rarely	Every month	Every week	Every day
1	3	5	7	10

How frequently do you have to spend time searching for 'lost' information?

Rarely	Every month	Once a week	Several times a week	Every day
1	3	5	7	10

How much time, on average, do you spend each day searching for information?

None	5 minutes	15 minutes	30 minutes	1 hour
1	3	5	7	10

How much time do you spend 'preparing' to work?

1 minute	10 minutes	15 minutes	30 minutes	1 hour
1	3	5	7	10

How long has the oldest paper been sitting on your desk?

1 day	3 days	1 weeks	2–3 weeks	Longer
1	3	5	7	10

How often do you procrastinate about a large or important project so that it turns into an emergency?

Never	Twice a year	Every couple of months	Every month	Very frequently
1	3	5	7	10

How often do you say that you are going to block off time 'catch up?'

Never	Couple of times a year	Every few months	Every month	Every week
1	3	5	7	10

control. After all, who created these feelings? We need to look no farther than at the person looking at us in the mirror.

Personal information management is very simple. Essentially it is a two-step process. First, you must know what your goals are, know what information you need and have a plan for where you are going to store information. Second, each time you finish looking at a computer file, paper or file, you must make a decision about where it should go and put it there.

About midway through implementing their PIM strategy, many clients will say, 'You know, this really isn't that difficult. I wonder why I had such a hard time doing this?' After a few moments' reflection they will then ask us how they got into this position. Not possessing a crystal ball, we then suggest reasons other clients have given us for being disorganised. After a few minutes' explanation, we turn the question back to them and ask why they think this problem developed. The reasons they offer typically fall into the categories below.

■ Procrastination: 'I'll do it later'

Probably half of the problems people experience with disorganisation could be eliminated if they understood one concept: *completion*. Most of what comprises the clutter commonly found in offices is the remnants of projects. While the work has been completed, the report read, or the final copy written, nothing was ever filed and the draft copies were not discarded.

Mail is one thing that usually does not get completed. How often do you look at your mail, glance at every item, and then pick out the important letters and put the non-important items to one side to be looked at later? Unfortunately the 'later' pile tends to build up and you have to spend a considerable amount of time sorting through it when you are implementing your PIM strategy. Instead, take 10–15 seconds to evaluate the letter in front of you and, if you do not need it, throw it away. Still more work lies on your desk to be done 'one of these days'. Unfortunately, 'one of these days' never comes, and the pile of work keeps getting higher. When you do get around to sorting through the piles, the information has 'spoiled', as often it is too late for you to take the necessary action.

■ Problems or situations that seem overwhelming

It is not easy operating in today's business environment. Recessions have cost many people sales or the loss of their job. Times have been very uncertain. A common response to this uncertainty is to ignore or avoid problems and difficult situations. Because paper (reports, letters, memos, applications and reading materials) is the tool of white-collar professionals, it is paper which gets ignored and ends up collecting on desks and tables.

One client, a saleswoman who had been ranked at the top of her office, was in danger of being fired. She had lost a very large account. She needed to find new business to replace this client, and time was of the essence. As you can imagine, she had a very high stress and anxiety level. As a result of this situation, she was behind on processing paperwork and filing important papers in client files. She was too overwhelmed to give these papers to her secretary because she thought something might still need to be done with them. Another outcome was that she was slow in making basic decisions. Thus the papers awaiting decisions were lying on her desk, and there were lots of them. Most of the decisions to be made were very simple.Many of the papers on her desk were easily dispatched to their correct location, which typically was to go to the department's administrative assistant. Others needed to be filed in client files. This could have been done when the item was dealt with, and would have taken only 10 seconds, but was not. Still on the desk was non-important mail and other non-important items that could have been thrown away when they were received but remained as evidence of her indecision.

Just organising your office and implementing a PIM strategy definitely will not rescue a failing business, nor will it increase your sales. However it will help you move towards those goals. One thing a PIM strategy will do is produce a clear list of what has and has not been done. Many people have been surprised to find out that the situation is not as bad as they anticipated after they actually took the time to set up a PIM strategy and see what work was really waiting for them. In fact, many of our clients have been quite relieved to realise that the work they actually must do is nothing like as large as the piles of paper would suggest.

A PIM strategy also *creates action*. Very often people who are stressed are spending all of their energy being stressed. Even the simple action of organising your information and getting rid of the irrelevant information and then deciding what items you are going to work on puts you into action. Once you are actively working you are not focused on being stressed, and you can begin to identify actions that will directly help you do what is necessary.

■ Too many organisational information systems

One client, who ran a small business, said he was the victim of too many organisation systems. Each time he hired a new office administrator or secretary she would come in and design her own system. Several secretaries later, what he left with was a collage of systems. At this point there is only one solution. The 'system' needs to be dismantled and then reconstructed. Having too many ways to keep track of information is just as bad as having no system.

■ Business growing rapidly: 'I'm just too busy'

A common reason people cite for not being organised is that they are too busy. The 'too busy' reason is the most frequent excuse given for a variety of situations that someone does not want to address. But for the person whose responsibilities and business have developed rapidly, becoming better organised is essential.

Instead of looking at a PIM strategy as something that 'uses up' time, look at it as a time investment and an opportunity to refocus yourself. As you sort through all of the important and urgent things that need to be done, take a look at what they are. Are there items in this group that can be delegated to someone else? Are there items that made sense at one point but are longer important in view of your increased business or responsibilities?

Many people base their judgement of being 'too busy' on the amount of paper on their desk. After you sort through these items, you will see how much of this paper goes into the bin, and how much of it stays on your desk as work that needs to be done.

▌ Unusual circumstances: 'I got behind' or 'It's been a busy ▌ time'

Some of our clients have stated that they have fallen behind, and consequently become disorganised, as a result of unusual circumstances or seasonal issues. Christmas or tax season are events that occur every year, and usually mean longer hours as well as letting more routine or non-urgent matters pile up. Other events, such as an illness, pull attention away from our work and leave us doing the minimum to get by while dealing only with very urgent matters.

We obviously cannot control the need to complete tax returns, or an illness, but we can control how we respond to the aftermath of the event. One client hired us to help her get organised after the illness, and eventual death, of her father. He lived out of town and she spent as much time with him as she could while still working. This went on for over six months. She handled the major responsibilities of her job but many of the less important items were ignored, and they ended up sitting on her desk.

If you find yourself in this situation, it is going to be very difficult to free enough time to set up a PIM strategy. Instead do what must be done and set a date to establish your PIM strategy when things return to normal. Select a date to do this even while you are busy. This way, once the commotion decreases, you have already scheduled a time for the PIM strategy.

■ Paperwork: 'I don't like paper and I don't like filing it'

Another commonly stated reason for disorganisation is that people do not like dealing with paper, nor do they like filing. However, for the white-collar professional, whether he or she 'likes' paper does not really matter. The fact is paper is part of the job and it must be dealt with. A PIM strategy can help you not to have to deal with papers. If you have a clear idea about which papers are important and which are not, those that are not important can go into the wastebasket and do not have to be dealt with again.

Filing problems are even easier to deal with. Filing is a 10-second job. When you have finished reviewing a document, spend 10 seconds filing it. These jobs are never listed on your to-do list, nor will you miss the ten seconds. While a common reaction to filing is procrastination, it is the worst way to deal with it. The 10-second filing operation never allows it to become a major activity.

■ Denial and avoidance: 'Problem, what problem?'

As with procrastination, some people develop problems in managing their information through denial of their existing problems. Instead of challenges being met head on, they tend to become buried at the bottom of the pile. We tell ourselves we will tackle the problem 'when we catch up', but that time never comes around.

One of the reasons we often do not want to get around to it is that, in the piles of paper on our desk, we have left traces and trails of unfinished work, as well as projects that often did not go the way we hoped. Many of these outcomes we consider as failures. So in addition to tackling the unpleasant chore of sorting through our information, we know that there are bombs lurking beneath the surface layer of papers. While avoiding these bad memories seems to handle the problem in the short term, it has long-term implications for us. As we let things build up, we can only expect our stress level to increase, not to mention the accompanying 'work' that is sitting on our desk.

▌ Where to start: 'I have a bad filing system' or 'I don't know how to set up a filing system'

As straightforward as setting up a filing system may sound, many people do not understand how to construct one. Nor do they understand how to combine the intricacies of setting up a system that accounts for both paper and computer files. So they go on with their work, without using any filing system, other than a few files in the filing cabinet. Computer files are often all in one place, without the benefit of directories that would make their retrieval quick and easy. When it comes to filing, it never gets done because they do not know where to put their files. Filing is an impossible task to manage unless you have a system.

The first thing that needs to be done in this situation is to set up a filing system. If you do not know how to do this, seek assistance from a friend, colleague, professional organiser or personal assistant. Once this system is in place, our clients are comfortable and even eager to file their important papers as they have a system that makes sense.

■ Lack of self-confidence: 'I have the answer here somewhere'

Many people are unsure of their abilities and want to cling to every bit of information, just in case they need it. Rather than having the confidence to remember minute details or, better, to know who to go to or where to look for the correct answer, people often want to save papers that they think will point them in the right direction. The only trouble with this strategy is that they may never be able to find what they need when they need it.

■ The 'pack rat' syndrome: 'I may need this some day'

Lack of clarity is probably one of the major reasons why people develop personal information management problems. If you are clear about what information you need, and you are careful to only save that information, your problems will probably be minimised even if your system is not the best. Instead of digging around in mountains of miscellaneous and unimportant information, if you have saved only the important information you need (even if it is randomly organised) you will still have some success in finding what you need. Much of what people save or file is not relevant: studies show that 80 per cent of what we save is never referred to again. Being clear about what you need and what you do not need will go a long way towards helping you work efficiently and in an organised manner.

The value of clarity was obvious with one client we worked with. This client, a finance director at a large multinational company, had a demanding job. As he was busy the number of papers on his desk and throughout the office increased to the point where he could not find anything. He called us to help him sort everything out. We began by explaining a few basic concepts to him about organisation and then found out what his problems were. Next we took a look at his current system, which was not too bad, except that he had a lot of information that was outdated and did not need to be kept. We went through his four filing cabinets, which were filled to capacity. When asked what files he still needed to keep, he took a quick look at each file, and without much hesitation decided what he needed and what he did not. Occasionally he would get stuck on a file and we would prompt him to make a decision. Then, as soon as he was puzzled about whether to keep a file, he considered the alternatives and within 30 seconds had reached a decision. This is what we mean by clarity. He was so clear about what he needed and what he did not need that the entire process of sorting through information and implementing his PIM strategy took only four hours.

Not everyone experiences the same clarity as the finance director. Another client took what typically would have been a six- or eight-hour process and spent 16 hours deciding what she needed and what she did not. Instead of making a decision within one minute about whether she needed something, she took three to ten minutes and would often start reminiscing or talk about something that was related to the paper she found. When that situation occurs, multiplied by hundreds of papers and files, it is easy to see why the time required to implement a PIM strategy increased drastically.

Yet sometimes people *sincerely* say they would like to become better organised, but still encounter problems. Everything seems important and has many potential uses. One term used to describe this type of person is a 'pack rat'.

Often this refers to collecting items within the home, but it definitely extends to offices. This can be a minor problem, such as keeping all books ever purchased, clothes that are too small or out of style, or saving all magazines. Warren and Ostrom in their 1988 *Psychology Today* article surveyed students, friends and colleagues who admitted their pack rat inclinations. When they were asked why they continued to save when there was no more space for what they had and they already had more of something than could ever be used, they gave four explanations which sounded logical enough: 'I might need this some time'; 'I'm sentimentally attached to it'; 'This might be worth something some day'; 'This is too good to throw away.'

On further questioning, the less logical reasons came out, such as the emotional upset and even physical illness caused by throwing things out. Feelings of loneliness, abandonment, regret, worry about throwing out something incorrectly or inability to decide what to throw out are all common reasons cited by pack rats for holding on to their possessions. While at home they may save clothes, books, magazines, dishes, memorabilia and papers, the syndrome also affects their offices (Warren and Ostrom, 1988, p.60). How can you tell if you are a pack rat or not? The answer is not clear-cut. Nearly everyone experiences some difficulty when it comes to parting with their papers and possessions. For some people it is mildly irritating or upsetting: they would rather not have to sort through everything, but they know they must and they do. At the other end of the spectrum are people who get extremely upset at throwing anything out and consequently avoid tackling this task. They avoid it to the extent that some rooms are filled to capacity and their books or magazines can be counted in the hundreds. Often there is so much paper you cannot even walk into the room.

Discarding items we no longer need is a necessary part of life. The reason is fairly simple. Examine your in-tray. Each day you get a stack of letters and magazines, as well as newspapers. Then there is internal mail, e-mail and reports that must be looked at and many of them saved. As we attend meetings or seminars we pick up additional papers. How quickly would our office fill up if we did not throw anything out? Or what if we threw out only a few items a week? After a while we would be bursting at the seams and would soon have to get a second office so we would have a place to work. It is like filling a jug of water. If you keep filling it, and never take the time to pour any into a glass and drink it, your jug will overflow. The same thing happens with office papers and computer files. However the dedicated pack rat will still claim that they have many 'valuable' papers, files and reference books. Some of these valuable items are:

- multiple copies of telephone directories (none of which is current);
- files between three and ten years old;
- old copies of newsletters, magazines and other information, from two to ten years old;
- office supplies well stocked enough to take care of an office (for several years);
- reference files for subjects long since abandoned or discontinued;
- catalogues and direct mail.

The list could go on forever, but you get the point. Basically, if you see value in items like these, and you are certain the information will be very useful 'one of these days', do not stop at your initial conclusion. Instead, ask yourself the following questions:

1. *When will I use this again?* If you can answer with a specific time or instance then you should keep the information.
2. *How will I use this information?* If you can answer with a specific project or scenario when you will need the information then it is good to keep it.
3. *In what situation will I use this again?* If you can name a specific situation when this information will be used again, then it is worth keeping. To determine what this situation is, ask yourself:
   (a) Where will I use this information again?
   (b) Why will I use this information again?
   (c) Who is going to ask for this information?

One note of caution. Unless you get specific answers to these questions, it means that the information goes into the 'one of these days' categories and should be discarded.

By now the die-hard pack rat is probably screaming: 'But you don't understand! This is really important.' We have worked with clients who have said the same thing, until we have asked how the papers will be used. The conversation goes something like this:

How will you use this?
Well, I do not know how, but I will need it.

When will you use this?
Well I don't exactly know. Actually I probably won't use this again.

Do you need to save this?
No I guess I don't need it.

Are you sure?

After a minute's consideration, the client does not come up with any reason for keeping it that is logical. It never fails. In all the years we have spent working with people, anywhere from 50 to 80 per cent of clients' papers and files end up in the bin. This occurs with their total agreement and consent. And often, towards the end of the day, they are throwing things out quicker than we are suggesting.

There are other variations of the pack rat syndrome that at one time were very wise. Many people who have trouble getting rid of excess information and belongings were told to 'save' things when they were a child. While this is an admirable notion, taken to extremes it is a problem. Innocent comments to children are often adopted as rules during adulthood. Another common difficulty is that people do not want to 'run out': never mind that for most of us whatever we run out of could be borrowed from a colleague, ordered for overnight delivery or purchased at numerous stores, many with late opening hours. People tend to stock up on office supplies, or many other personal items, as if they were going to open a shop. The trouble is that all of these items will be old and dusty by the time they are used. And, instead of using this stockpile, the same people are probably going to the store and buying more.

Another pack rat characteristic is frugality. People will often dive into the wastebasket after a paper clip, or save every envelope they receive. All of these habits have a useful function, but if you are spending more time retrieving these items than the value of your time justifies, you are being 'penny wise and pound foolish' and, if you have saved hundreds of these items, when will you use them? Remember, landfills can be found either at the county dump or in your office. Which do you prefer?

▍Reasons that prompt the implementation of a PIM strategy

These reasons are the ones that clients often say have caused their disorganisation. However it is important to note that all of these reasons can be overcome. We continually deal with people who decide that they are going to take control of their office and become more organised. When that happens, nothing is going to stop them. Clients decide that they are no longer going to put up with their disorganisation and state their commitment to developing and implementing their PIM strategy. With determination they can resolve their problems.

CHAPTER 10

Beginning to implement your personal information management strategy

You can now implement your PIM strategy. It is not much more difficult than putting your groceries away. The first crucial step is to have a clear idea of what your goals are. Secondly, you must know what information you need to achieve those goals. Finally, you must know what tools you want to use to manage the information. For the person who has not been managing his information, and has been letting everything collect with the statement 'I'll take care of that later', beginning will be the most difficult part.

When the process of putting the PIM strategy into place begins, the chances are that your office will be filled with lots of files, loose papers and computer files. There are two different ways to begin approaching this project. Neither is better: you must decide which one will work best for you.

■ The macro approach

The macro approach implements the PIM strategy in one or two sessions, which may occupy most of the day (or, in the case of one our colleagues, six hours, from 6 pm to midnight!). For some people this approach works because they can concentrate fully on the job at hand and restrict the process to one day. This method has several advantages:

- you can concentrate fully on the job in hand for one day;
- you can declare an 'emergency' and focus your efforts on one project;
- one day creates pressure to get the job completed;
- you have maximum motivation for continuing, especially when it looks much easier to stop.

To use this approach, take your list of important areas and decide where files should go. The files that you use most frequently, or those that are the primary focus of your job, should go in the location that is the closest and most accessible to you. Then individual papers, computer files and other bits of information can be put into their respective places.

This approach may be characterised as 'tearing down with a rapid build-up'. By this we mean that, when the project is started, everything is examined and either discarded or placed in the appropriate file, which may be newly created. The way the office looks at the beginning of the day and the way it will look at the end are completely different. As we have worked with clients, some of them have approached ecstasy as the top of their desk becomes visible and the bin becomes fuller. While beginning the process was not the most interesting thing they could think of to do, they became more enthusiastic as the sorting out process moved forward and they could see their accomplishments. Such clients certainly benefit from the macro approach of doing it all at once. One client was even rewarded for his efforts by finding a bottle of wine that was buried beneath many unnecessary papers in his credenza.

■ The micro approach

Another approach, the micro approach, is a 'creation' approach. This means that, while the basic structure and necessary elements are in place, the PIM strategy is created and formed piece by piece. For those people whose eyes glaze over when they contemplate doing this project all at once, and who are certain they do not have a whole day available to devote to this project, the micro approach will be effective. For this to work best there must already be some structure for information in place, whether it is filing cabinets or software. All the decisions about what information is important must be made. They are just made at a number of different times rather than all at once. The implementation of your PIM strategy is done in an incremental fashion and may take a month before it is complete.

Using the micro approach puts all the pieces of information in place one piece at a time. For instance, the contents of one file drawer or one file folder may be evaluated and organised in accordance with the PIM strategy. One file, or perhaps one file drawer, will be evaluated during a day, and that is all that will be done. The micro approach will take a long while, but it is one way to complete the project for the person who is extremely short of time.

To use this approach you should decide what the goal for each day is. Is it spending 15 minutes a day to organise one file or one desk drawer? To keep yourself on schedule, make a commitment to do one drawer or two to three files a day. If necessary, establish a schedule and display it next to your calendar. This project must be given a high priority, or it is not likely to be completed.

Scenario: an architect implementing his personal information management strategy

To understand more clearly how to implement your PIM strategy, let us watch as an architect begins to do this for himself. We will use this scenario to illustrate some of the most important concepts in developing and implementing your PIM strategy.

To set up his system, our architect spends some time considering what the important areas of his job are. From this information he decides what files he needs most. He decides that his most important information is his *client* files. Also very important is his file on *good architectural business practices* that contains useful articles taken from professional journals. He determines that his *expense report* file, an *Architects' Association* file and a *Christmas party* file are also important. He decides to keep his client files in one place, and that place should be the top two drawers of his filing cabinet. He collects the client files that are around his office and begins putting them in the filing cabinet in alphabetical order. This will work well, as his co-workers can also have access to files they need. He gets to the Hs. The *Hanson* file is for a client whose project was finished last year. He pulls that out and puts it on the desk of his administrative assistant, who will file it in the central filing room. Then he looks at the *Smith* file. That should go to his colleague, as his work is finished and his colleague needs to begin working on it. He puts the file in his co-worker's office. Several more client files are moved to the central filing room. This makes available more room than he expected. All of the client files are now organised and are exactly where they belong. His office also looks neater, as many of the files that were lying around were taking up space long after the work was complete.

In his desk drawer he keeps other important files such as articles on good architectural business practices (he aspires to partner level), his expense report file, including both completed copies and blank forms, and the Architects' Association file, which holds necessary papers as well as the current newsletter. He also has a file for the Christmas party because he is in charge of planning it this year. However there are other files in his desk drawer that he is not quite sure about. He pulls one out. It appears to be old company memos from 1991 to 1994. He leafs through the file and, after a few moment's reminiscence, decides there is no reason why he should have these files and throws them away.

This architect now has the basics of his PIM strategy in place: the client files in the filing cabinet and his administrative files in his desk drawer. Yet there are still many loose pieces of paper lying around. Next he turns to the papers on his credenza. Papers are scattered everywhere, and the piles are high. He picks up the first sheet of paper. It is a copy of an expense form, for which he has already received payment. This should go into his *expense report* file. He files it there in about five seconds. Next he picks up the daily newspaper from three days ago:

Well, that would have been interesting to read, but I guess it isn't too important now and I don't have time to look at it anyway. If I want to read a paper I will read today's paper, which I have in my briefcase. He puts the old newspaper in the bin. He picks up another piece of paper. It is a company memo saying that the office carpeting will be cleaned this weekend. The trouble is 'this weekend' was a month ago. That goes into the bin. Next he finds the drafts of an important letter he sent to a client. The final copy was filed in the client file, and the draft papers now belong in the waste bin. He files some more client documents and then discards old memos and direct mail that he was going to look at 'one of these days'. He begins to see the surface of the credenza: *I guess these papers weren't as important as I thought, but I know I still have some very important papers.*

He continues going through the papers. He finds several letters from clients that should have been filed in their respective files. He takes 30 seconds, walks over to the filing cabinet, and puts those papers into their respective files. He is glad he found those papers and filed them. *The rest of this stuff is pretty worthless.* He systematically looks at each piece of paper and either files it or discards it.

Now he turns to his desk, which has the most important and current papers on it. It is still covered with many papers which he thinks cannot be thrown out. He proceeds to go through the desk papers one by one. As he does this he decides to count just how many are important, and how many end up in the bin. As he looks at each paper, he wonders where they should have been and why he is spending time doing this. He considers stopping at this point, because the papers on top of his desk probably represent work that he is going to have to do on Monday. However he continues, and here are the results:

Waste bin	61%
Need to file	25%
Work to do	6%
Give to assistant/colleague	5%
Take home	2%
Read	1%

Of the 109 pieces of paper or groups of paper on the desk, seven pieces represented work that needed to be done the following morning. Everything else fitted into the above categories. Most notable was that 61 per cent of the papers went into the wastebasket.

This was a sobering discovery. All this time he had been looking at his desk and had been overwhelmed by the amount of paper, and therefore the amount of work, that was facing him. He was amazed that he could easily throw away 61 per cent of the papers on top of his desk because the information was now unimportant. At this point he really wished he had thrown it away as he went along. It could have saved him a lot of time.

■ Much more than clearing the desk

It is important to note that what the architect is doing is much more methodical and complex than just 'clearing his desk'. Clearing the desk produces a clean desk that will probably last for one or two days. Or, as some of our more sceptical clients say, one or two hours. However creating a PIM strategy and continuing to maintain it creates the structure and the ability to always be able to manage your information and retrieve anything effortlessly.

■ Satisfaction of completing the job

At 4 pm, after the architect finished implementing the PIM strategy, he looked around and was amazed at what he did not see. He did not see papers stacked on his credenza, desk and on the floor; he did not see client files propped up against the filing cabinet; on his desk were only the papers that needed his immediate attention on Monday morning.

As he looked at his office, he was very happy and considered his day's work to be a major accomplishment. By concentrating and keeping his focus, he completed implementing his PIM strategy in one day. He also knew that he did more than just clean up his office. He created a structure for retaining, as well as discarding, information. Furthermore, because he was clear about what he needed and what he did not need, he knew he would be able to maintain the structure as he went along and would not need to spend another day like today.

He also had some insights into the way he dealt with his mail. He always looked at the important materials that came from clients. However he tended to let the less important mail pile up. He would spend time after 5 pm looking at that. However today he spent a lot of time going through the less important mail and realised that it was not *less* important – it had *no* importance. Most of the less important mail went into the bin, but there were a couple of things that he wished he had looked at sooner. One was a postcard reminding him of a networking meeting which was held two weeks earlier. That would have been an important piece of mail to look at when it came, but it was sitting in the 'mail to be read' pile. The other thing he wished he had seen was an advertisement for an architects' seminar in three weeks. He wanted to attend that and he sent in his registration. However he ended up paying an extra $50 for a late registration fee. Not looking at the mail cost him $50 at the very least, not to mention his valuable time today.

This situation is a perfect example of Covey's assertion that 20 per cent of the work provides 80 per cent of the value. The less important mail that the architect sorted through is a prime example of taking time to do the 80 per cent that only produces 20 per cent of the value. It would have been more beneficial for the architect if he had discarded the mail he did not need as it arrived each day.

■ Some important information storage concepts

- *Action/work in progress*. This is work that must be done 'now'. 'Now' can be defined as today or within the next few days. This information needs immediate attention and basically makes up the to-do list.
- *Active storage*. Active storage represents information that resides in your office. It represents work that has been completed and is being retained for future reference. This information is not on a to-do list.
- *Archive storage*. This is information that must be saved to satisfy company requirements or legal requirements. It may be old financial information, copies of tax returns, old client files or anything else that has value. It should be away from the active storage area.

So far, the architect has focused on the active storage area and the archive storage area. This was the information that had got out of hand and was creating the cluttered look of the office. Too often the storage information was getting mixed up with the work that required immediate attention. This was creating the information searches that lasted 30 minutes or more.

Once the active storage and archive storage areas were organised, the architect could begin to see that he actually had a lot more space in which to do his work. Then he began to create a filing structure for his work in progress. He did not believe in having a totally clear desk and found that it was most effective to put urgent things on the right side of his desk. After clearing out the desk drawer that held hanging files, he found he had plenty of room for other files. What he wanted to do was put the three most active client files in his desk drawer: when he received calls from those clients, he could retrieve their files immediately. There was also the matter of storing large drawings. He found that by putting these drawings in a corner to the right of his credenza they were out of sight yet accessible, and he could conveniently retrieve them.

There are many questions that may be occurring to you now, and they probably fit into these main categories: How much time is required for this process? What information should be saved? How much information should you save? Where should files be placed?

■ How much time did the architect spend on this project?

Because he had a good idea of what information was important before he started, the architect was able to go through this process fairly rapidly. He spent seven hours from start to finish. Of course, this time was spent exclusively on organising his office. He did not take any time to actually do work, or to answer the phone (which was quiet on a Saturday). Seven hours is a fairly average time to implement a PIM strategy. The fastest we have seen is four hours. If you agonise over the decisions of whether to keep something, or become stuck during the process, you can expect to spend double that time setting up your PIM strategy. Also times vary according to the amount of information, the size of the office and the speed of the person doing the work.

The architect began the process on a Saturday morning, after a good night's sleep. This was a time when no one was in the office, nor were any clients calling. He began at about 9 am and finished the job at 4 pm. While he had spent most of his Saturday doing this project, he knew he would recoup the time he spent within one week, as he could leave his office at 5 o'clock most nights, instead of staying until 6 pm or 7 pm to 'catch up on paperwork'. Also he was looking forward to not wasting any more time hunting for the papers he needed. Last week he spent 35 minutes looking for a letter a client had sent him during the previous week. With episodes like that, there was no way he was going to be efficient and effective enough to be promoted.

If the time commitment appears too great, consider this. Most people spend at least 20 to 45 minutes a day looking for lost papers. If the time is not actually spent looking for papers, it is often spent worrying that you may not be able to find what you need. Determine how much time you spend looking for things in your office. Divide that number into the estimated time that you think it will take to implement your PIM strategy. You will be surprised at just how quickly the payback comes.

■ How long should you keep information?

There is no single right answer to this question. Instead, when developing the PIM strategy, each person should determine how long to retain information. Once you have answered the question, you can make future decisions about keeping information. For most people, keeping their own administrative files for one to two years is sufficient, although it will vary according to your circumstances. After that time the information is often too old and not useful. However the files themselves may be useful year after year. For instance, a file for information on a networking group will be useful as long as you are participating. What will not be useful is information in it that is more than a year old. For some, six months is sufficient, while other people will feel more comfortable keeping their files for one to three years. Whatever time frame is chosen, as long as the information remains valuable to you then the time frame is correct.

In the case of the architect, because the client files were company property, he gave the completed files to the administrative assistant who filed them in the central filing room. Files that he created, which were his own administrative files, were handled differently. He decided that, if some project or idea file had not been used in the last year and would not be used again, he would get rid of it.

These guidelines relate to files and information that we create that are not required by our company or by the government. Many central government laws govern how long records should be kept for businesses. While we might like to discard old tax records, they should be saved for seven to ten years, and in some cases even longer. To find out how long you should save your financial records, ask your accountant. Financial records may include such items such as client invoices, accounts payable invoices and bank statements.

For any business or individual working in certain areas covered by US federal regulations, there are record retention guidelines that are required by law. The details of these requirements are contained in a 100-plus page publication from the US government, called *Guide to Record Retention Requirements*. The UK government specifies that VAT – or sales tax records – must be kept for six years. This is why the question, 'How long should I keep my records?' is not a simple one to answer. For legal documents, ask your solicitor how long you should retain the records. He can advise you according to the specific details in your case.

One important caveat. Just because documents have to be kept, this does not mean that they should be among your working files. In fact the opposite is the case. While this information must be kept, it should be in a storage area away from your current information. A box that is clearly labelled, in your archive storage area, can be retrieved easily if the information is ever needed.

■ What information do you keep?

Our architect implemented his PIM strategy without too much confusion or trouble. That is because, first, he had a very clear idea about what information he needed to keep. He developed a list of his necessary files beforehand as part of his PIM strategy. He considered what he really needed carefully before beginning the implementation of the project. Second, when he came across a paper that did not fit within the files he listed for his PIM strategy, he considered for a few seconds whether he needed it. Third, his list of files was not set in stone: as he was going through the files on his credenza, he realised that he definitely needed a file that contained information on computer-aided design, so he added it.

To determine what information you need to keep, ask yourself the following questions, 'Do I need this?' and 'Will I ever use it again?' If the answer is a resounding 'no', your action is very straightforward. If, however, you may want to use this information again, you should ask yourself *when* and *in what circumstances*. If you do not get a clear answer to those questions, this is something that you really are not going to need again.

■ Why should you get rid of information?

The answer is of course, because you will never use the information again, for example when someone else is responsible for the project, or it is their primary job to store information and you were just given copies. The estimates vary, but 75 to 90 per cent of the papers we save are never referred to again. From our experience, even those most protective about discarding information readily concede that about 50 per cent of what they have can be discarded, after considering each individual paper or file on its merits. For people more willing to discard old information, they usually find that about 80 per cent of what they are saving is unnecessary. Remember that, just because paper has been put into a binder or file, this does not mean that it needs to become a permanent part of your office.

■ Reasons to save papers that are not immediately pertinent

If you think you might need a file or project papers for something you will do in the future, hold on to the file, but take one minute to leaf through it and determine what information must be saved. Nine copies of last year's Christmas menu are not really necessary. One is sufficient. While the file may be needed, perhaps not all the papers within it are necessary.

For an *event* file, working papers that contain notes about arrangements or thoughts on potential ways to do something that were not used, are not needed. Nor is information about vendors or options that were discarded from last year's event.

■ How much should you save?

People make problems for themselves through the mistaken belief that they must keep information because 'I may need this some day.' In fact, if this is your sole reason for keeping something, it is probably your best clue that it probably will not be needed again. On the other hand, if you can say, 'I will need this again,' then that statement justifies keeping the information. While you can retain information you may need one day, if you do not have enough storage space, or if you continually have to hunt through it to find what you do need, then it is costing you more than its future value.

Examples of information that are saved in anticipation of the need for it 'one of these days' are old office memos, two-year-old class schedules to remind you what courses are offered, old association newsletters and many other miscellaneous pieces of information. Here are some categories of information that more often than not end up being discarded (or can be discarded):

- magazines over six months old;
- files containing projects that have been completed or discarded (other than a concluding report, if it might be used again);
- direct mail, catalogues and other unsolicited mail that was going to be read as soon as time was available: as the dates on it become older and older, it ends up being thrown away without being read;
- rough drafts of letters or documents that have already been sent out;
- professional journals still in the plastic wrapping when there is no time to read them;
- old bills not needed for tax or expense payments;
- clippings and advertisements outlining projects or 'fun' activities that were going to be done 'one of these days' but never have been. When you have time to schedule something, you can think about what you would like to do and then make a call to get the current details.

While this is a brief listing, it gives you an idea of the kinds of information that will not be important. When people hold on to out-of-date files or information, it may signify more serious underlying problems. Sometimes project papers are retained long after the project has been abandoned by themselves or has been rejected by management. Often holding on to this information signifies more than just a failure to discard a file. Each time they see that file, or that paper, they are reminded of a lost battle or a perceived failure. If something negative has happened to you, learn the necessary lessons and move on. Do not hold on to the remnants of the loss, as it will only serve as a reminder of failure. Who needs any extra reminders of failure or things that did not work out?

■ Some information retention strategies

There are several different strategies that people adopt to deal with the amount of information that should be saved. One style is *super-streamlined*. This is used by a person who believes in keeping only the absolute minimum of papers and files. Paper goes into the wastebasket just as quickly as it arrives and the information is remembered. Once a project is finished, the accompanying papers, except for the final document, are discarded. This person has a good idea what to do in the future, and knows that no two projects are exactly the same: each has its own characteristics, and each is created as needed, instead of old files being looked at. (This is in fact the personal style for both of the present authors – we keep completely clear desks, all of the time, only keeping documents for the absolute minimum of time, and routinely discarding any information that is out of date.)

Another style is *streamlined*. This is used by a person who has the pertinent information he needs, plus other information that will be useful 'one of these days'. The information that is not readily used now is well organised and labelled so that, when it is needed, it can be found.

The third style is *well-stocked*. This type of person, while he has important information, also has a large supply of reference material and interesting information that in most cases will not be needed again. But in the one instance that it is needed, he will have it. One of his greatest joys is being able to retrieve an esoteric document that he has been holding in anticipation of a future need. Of course he has hundreds of other documents that will never be needed again.

■ Where should your files be placed?

Important or frequently used files should be close to you. If you have to walk across the room, or even to another room, to file something that you frequently use, your inclination is going to be not to file it. Files should be in a cabinet or drawer that works properly and is easy to open. If you have to struggle with a drawer to open it, you will not want to bother with it and items that should be filed will not be, because the drawer is troublesome.

Files should not be crowded in a drawer. If they are, they will be difficult to get at and the result will be that things will not be filed. Better to spend a few minutes weeding out unnecessary information so that, when you do need to file something, the filing job is not get listed on the to-do list because it includes sorting through the drawer's contents. In the case of our architect, because there were some files that he seemed to use every day, he put them in his desk drawer so they could be produced within seconds.

■ How do you arrange your files?

Most of your primary files will be placed close to you. They will be in a desk drawer or hanging files, or they will be in a nearby filing cabinet. There are two approaches for arranging these files. One is to put them in alphabetical order. The other is to arrange them according to their importance, or frequency of use. This latter approach relies on your ability to remember where each file is located. If that works for you, fine. (This is your personal information, not information that is used by the entire department.)

Other people have used a numbering system. This works by creating numbered files – assigning a number to each. In order to find the relevant file, you have to look at the file list and find its number. Each file is arranged in numerical order. For the person who has difficulty remembering what name might have been used to file something under, this method has certain advantages. For one thing, several key words and a brief description can be used to describe the file, giving more flexibility. This could appeal to someone who is number-oriented, and might be easier than remembering names of files.

■ Where do you find what you filed?

Many books have been written about the different methods to enhance your memory. However there are some simple steps which will ensure that you will be able to retrieve the information you need. One is to think about how you will ask for the information again. A minute's reflection in most cases will give you the best name to use so you remember the file when it is needed. If you can name the file according to the context in which it will be referred to again, it is likely you will be able to remember it.

The next step is to use four of your senses to reinforce where you are putting a file. If you are afraid you will not be able to find your marketing file again, put it in the spot where you want it to be and spend 30 seconds saying where the file is, looking at it, touching it and hearing where you are saying it is. While using your senses to recall where a file is may seem like a simple technique, it is effective.

As far as possible, leave your information and important items in the same spot. For instance, if you always seem to be searching for your calendar or cheque-book, have it reside in your top left desk drawer. As soon as you have this place fixed firmly in your mind, you will need to make sure that these items are returned to that drawer after use. As soon as you develop this habit it will be useful. For instance, how often do you need to search for the milk?

Basically our brains process information in many different ways. Some people are more visual, others focus on sound and still others see words. Using your senses to help you remember information will ensure that you are able to find that information again.

■ Using visual clues

Colour is another way of helping you to remember where your information is. Human memory is very flexible and can relate to information in many ways using different cues (Cole, 1982, p. 62). For some people, colour coding files into broad categories makes the files interesting and pleasing to look at. It also facilitates the retrieval of files since the colour, the name and positioning give three suggestions about where the file is. One client decided to put her to-do files in a pastel shade of pink. This colour was pleasing and gave her a feeling of calmness that combated her anxiety about the amount of work that needed to be done. Another client put his files into four broad categories, financial, clients, administrative and marketing, and assigned a colour to each.

Another way people remember where they have put information is to 'see' where that information is. For example, they would think of the file that they want, and then create a mental picture of where the file is. To see if you remember like this, pick out a file and try to recall where it is. How did you remember? Did you see a picture of its location in your mind? Or did you think, 'Second drawer in the filing cabinet'? If you formed pictures, you are visually oriented; if the words 'second drawer filing cabinet' came to mind, then you are more word-oriented. Putting files in filing cabinets or away inside other containers should not be a problem for you as you remember where it is by 'thinking in words'. Many of our clients are extremely visually oriented. They see pictures of where things are. To be able to see pictures, the papers and files must be laid out visually. Filing cabinets are not at all visual. It is virtually impossible to visualise where a file is inside the filing cabinet. While many of our visually oriented clients have filing cabinets, it is not surprising that they are mostly empty and the important papers are out where they can be seen.

Visual memory can compensate for a lack of organisation in filing systems but it only works if the amount of important papers is small. Six items arranged on a desk will be recalled solely through visual memory and their presence will easily prompt you to conduct the work that they refer to. If you have 60 items on your desk (many people have this many) visual cues will disappear, and the important items on your desk will 'disappear'.

■ The importance of a clear desk

A clear desk is not a goal, it is rather a tool to help you do your work. One of the most simple and 'cleanest' systems to prompt you to do work is to put something on your desk. If you have six items, you can clearly see what needs to be done and arrange them in the order of their importance. In fact the 'finding' function of a desk is as important as the 'reminding' function, – according to a desk organisation study conducted by Thomas W. Malone (Malone, 1983, pp.99–112).

The best strategy for people who are visually oriented is to clear out all of their unnecessary papers and then create an information storage system that allows for the most visual recall of information possible. This may involve using a second desk or table, or using vertical file holders to stand information up on shelves so it is in clear view.

Yet another reason for having a clear desk is to prevent work of medium importance from being overlooked. In Malone's study, two of the four people who classified themselves as 'messy' said that sometimes medium importance items 'slipped through the cracks' and did not get done. None of the people with a neat office had this problem, Malone's study demonstrated. The objective of a clear desk is not a clean desk. Rather it is to allow you to use your desk as a tool to prompt you about what urgently needs to done.

A PIM strategy is not intended to increase the complexity of your filing system. Instead it is meant to make things easier so you can instantly retrieve what you need. In fact, for most people, there is a general lack of motivation towards the upkeep of elaborate filing systems: the less time spent filing the better (Cole, 1982, p.60). So anything that can show you what needs to be done with little effort or complexity is likely to be a success.

■ If you can't find a file or paper

No matter how organised or methodical you are about maintaining your information storage system, at some point you will probably misplace a paper or file. To locate it again, try the following steps:

1. See if the paper was misfiled in the files in front of or behind the place where it should have been.
2. See if the paper accidentally fell into the bottom of the filing cabinet or between files.
3. Remember when you last had the paper or file. Where was it? What were you doing? Often papers can be misfiled by mistake, especially if you have several projects and files on your desk at one time.

If all of these steps fail, ask any colleagues who might have used or moved it if they have seen the paper or file. Then if you still have not found it, you can do one of two things: you can begin working on something else, as quite often files and lost papers turn up eventually; or, if you need it immediately, you must conduct a logical, methodical search, going through everything in your office.

Lost papers and files are one good reason to restrict the number of files and projects that are out on your desk at any one time (or even that are filed neatly). When accidents do happen and you have to search through your papers and files, the fewer there are to search, the easier it is.

■ Use your brain to store information

Finally one thing that people do not give themselves credit for is the importance of their brain. Often, when people save everything, they do so because they are afraid that they will forget something. Nothing could be further from the truth. We only use 0.1 per cent or less of our brain's capabilities. The human brain far surpasses any computer in terms of its complexity and versatility. Few people have ever been taught how to get the most from their brains: while children were told to memorise facts, they were not taught how the brain works and how they could best work with their brain (Russell, 1979, p.7).

But beyond spending time attempting to learn better memory techniques, there are other ways to use your brain to store information. People will save bits of information or tear out articles from magazines or newspapers to remind them of an idea or an activity they may want to do. When they do this they fail to appreciate that reading the article, and concentrating on it during the time they are reading it, will provide them with the information when the time comes for them to remember, for example, that computer classes were offered at the community centre, or that the local library will have the information they may need. Then they can call the community centre or library and get the correct details.

CHAPTER 11

Maintaining your personal information management strategy

If you do not maintain your information strategy, you will soon find that piles of paper will build up again, probably pretty rapidly. The truth of this statement is seen vividly with the example of Marks & Spencer. In the late 1950s, Marks & Spencer started its war against paper bureaucracy and succeeded in eliminating 26 million forms and reduced its staff from 27 000 to 20 000. The effort was spearheaded by top management and was assumed to be successful.

As impressive as these results were, they did not last. In 1973, under the chairmanship of Sir Marcus Sieff, Marks & Spencer had to conduct a second campaign, called 'Good Housekeeping' At this stage, staffing levels had again built up to 27 000. They were reduced again, to 26 000, by not filling posts as employees left. M&S efforts also produced many gains by drastically reducing the numbers of forms that were used. One of the gains cited was with a returned merchandise form, which resulted in an alternative procedure that eliminated the form (13 million annually) and provided better and faster service to the customer (Rayner, 1975, pp.8–14).

Just doing a thorough job did not mean it was the end of the story for Marks & Spencer. It is the same for you. Just because your PIM strategy is implemented, this does not mean that is the last time you need to go through your files and eliminate unnecessary information. Like the groceries that are eventually eaten, your PIM strategy requires continual replenishing so that you can always have the right amount of information at your fingertips. In the following paragraphs we offer some simple ways to help you keep your PIM strategy up to date.

■ File audit

This will need to be done every six months or, at the minimum, once a year. It is necessary because, as projects end or priorities change, the information that relates to them becomes irrelevant. Also information is saved in anticipation of events happening or projects being done. Once the events have passed, this information ages quickly and begins to take up space that could be put to better use.

Even if you went through all your files as you implemented your PIM strategy, your efforts will only be useful for about six months. After that point, unnecessary papers will build up in your files as issues and information become irrelevant and unimportant. Instead of taking several hours, a file audit should only take a minute. You can go through all files at one time, or you can do a file as you finish using it. To audit a file, go through it discarding the rough drafts or papers that are not useful any longer. Keep only the relevant information. When you use this file again, you will have the papers that are pertinent and you will not be using up valuable filing space.

■ Completion

Another key ingredient to maintaining your PIM strategy is completion. This is a very simple concept that is often forgotten in our haste to move on to the next project. Completion means putting away (filing) all of the papers and materials connected with a project. Information management occurs with one piece of information or one computer file at a time. No more and no less: once you have an established information management system in place, the key to retaining it is putting one paper or one file away at a time.

As we mentioned earlier, another part of a successful personal information management strategy is *practice*. Just spending one day implementing your PIM strategy is not sufficient. Instead you must continually replace files and papers that you have used back in their place. Otherwise, they will begin to pile up again and the value of the PIM strategy will decrease.

Completion also occurs in smaller steps. For instance, at the end of the day, take five to ten minutes to put away papers you are finished with and get prepared for what needs to be done the next day.

■ Ten-second filing operation

One reason people give for not filing away their information is that they do not have any time to do this. However it takes only ten seconds to file a piece of paper or to put a file back into the drawer. Filing the finished product at the end of the task provides several benefits. Firstly the filing operation never reaches your to-do list. This is a very important reason not to put off filing a file or piece of paper. One paper or file takes approximately ten seconds to file, but letting papers pile up exponentially increases the time needed to file them. That task becomes another item on the to-do list which is probably already overflowing.

Second, filing your materials away one completion of a job provides a physical action that gives you a solid sense of completing the task. While this may not sound important, for people whose work takes the form of ideas or concepts, having something physical to do to complete the task gives more evidence that work was completed. People accustomed to working with their hands, or producing or manufacturing a product, already have a solid sense of completion when the finished product sits in front of them.

Some people remark that filing is a task that should be left to their secretary, but if everything is filed immediately after you have finished using it, then it is not much of a task. You would not ask your secretary to turn the pages of a report you are reading. Why would you ask her to file one piece of paper that belongs in your desk drawer?

■ Learn to make split-second decisions

One of the most difficult things for people when implementing a PIM strategy is making split-second decisions about whether they should keep a paper or computer file. Once the PIM strategy is developed and put into place, then it is a matter of taking a few seconds to determine if each individual piece of paper should be filed or discarded.

Agonising over a decision does not produce a better decision, and yet that is what some people tend to do. They are afraid of making the wrong decision, or afraid that they will really need something. Besides producing frustration and indecision, this has another major effect which is even worse. Afraid of making a wrong decision, people will stop making any decisions at all. Papers will pile up, in anticipation of being filed or dealt with 'one of these days'. Then the effectiveness of your PIM strategy will be totally defeated.

■ 'I'll do it later'

This is a statement that will certainly be the downfall of your carefully crafted personal information management strategy. 'I'll do it later' is usually a guarantee of not doing it at all.

■ Create your conceptual tools

These are something you can create which enable you instantly to know what to do with information that arrives. You can have categories of information which you automatically pass on to a subordinate, or other information that is discarded because it is not central to your job.

■ Re-engineer your information management

Too often people hold on to information because it arrives, not because they need it. Instead of keeping information because someone sends it to you, keep it only if it is important to what you are doing. Re-engineer your process of retaining information so that it makes the most sense for what you need, according to your goals.

■ Managing daily information flow

The previous suggestions address what to do about information that is already in your office. But what do you do with information that arrives each day, and seems to stack up more quickly than you can deal with it?

■ The white-collar production line

White collar employees and managers' work is similar to a production line. The main difference is that the parts are paper and the tools are desktop computers and pens. Work and information is received through many different mediums, and the information needs to be utilised and acted upon before any results can be obtained. If the information, and thus the work, creates a bottlenecked by sitting on your desk for a lengthy period this results in lost productivity.

The key to keeping work moving is to act upon items as quickly and promptly as possible. Some projects obviously cannot be done in a half hour, yet many *can* be done that quickly. When implementing your PIM strategy for clients, often what we find on their desks are not huge, long-term projects. Instead there is a collection of items that co-workers have forwarded to them for their consideration or for information. Often the collection may include mail or other items that involve a decision to attend a seminar or order a product. While a split-second decision cannot always be made, a decision must still be made quickly so that the production line does not come to a complete stop.

To take the production line image further, an office's raw materials are letters, reports and e-mail. They are stored until they are needed (in the 'work in progress' section or in 'active storage'). As with a manufacturing line, when the stock gets to a low level materials are sent to the manufacturing line for their use. The white-collar production line stores letters and other information until you begin working on the project.

One other important piece of wisdom may be gleaned from a production line. Whatever product is being manufactured, one thing is certain: only one product is produced at a time. While the line may be stopped and retooled in order to produce something else, only one product comes off the line at any one time. Contrast this situation with that of white-collar workers who have ten things on their desk at once. Amongst this is the one project that actually commands their attention. The fact is, you can only write, read or think about one thing at a time. Many people are trying to operate their production line and produce several things at once. No wonder we are experiencing stress and exhaustion.

A final important lesson is provided by the manufacturing operation's storage of materials for 'work in progress'. These parts and materials are carefully labelled and organised so they can be retrieved instantly when they are needed. Otherwise, expensive machine time and employee time will be wasted if these materials have to be searched for before they can be used. Can you imagine a factory with hundreds of parts and materials all lumped together? Retrieving any needed material would require digging through the pile. Yet this is the situation many white-collar employees put themselves in by leaving different projects strewn all over their office. If we remember the earlier brief discussion of 'just-in-time' manufacturing, we can see that many of the concepts discussed there, such as only having just enough materials in storage to produce what you need at the moment, also apply.

Here is how you begin to construct your 'work in progress/waiting' area. This may be one side of your desk, an in-box or a credenza. It is a clearly designated place to put information that cannot be immediately dealt with. Many time management experts advocate having only one thing on a desk at a time. While this rule may seem useful, in reality it is not terribly practical. The key to making this system work is scheduling *time* to do the work. If something arrives that requires five minutes or less of time, do it right away and get it out of your 'work in progress/waiting' area.

The 'work in progress/waiting' idea also seems to have some degree of support from work on the psychology of memory which has found, as we discussed earlier, that people have a 'short-term memory, which stores things to be processed (telephone numbers, names, addresses, for example). It seems that supporting short-term memory by using what might be called a 'memory prosthesis' or 'memory aid' (in the form of a 'work in progress/waiting' area) removes some of the mental burden of managing information. (The idea of computers as 'memory prostheses' is currently being developed by Rank Xerox at their research laboratory in Cambridge, England. They are developing a series of software and hardware devices that allow users to look at records of events they have experienced to support the act of managing information and recalling important information.) In his book, *Things That Make Us Smart*, Don Norman says that perceptual and spatial representations are more natural and are preferred to non-perceptual representations, but only if the mapping between the two objects is clear (Norman, 1993, p.72). So, in the case of our architect, seeing blueprints standing up against the wall will work better than an elaborate storage system that removes them from his view.

■ Activate your production line

For many people work begins when they receive information. This could be letters, e-mail, reports, memos, phone calls or faxes. This work requires that they read the material and then act upon it.

■ Decide what can be discarded

From the viewpoint of the production line, after this information is received, there is one initial decision to be made: *Do you keep the information or do you discard it?* This is a very important decision to make and one that will help your PIM strategy to be successful. Much of the mail you receive can go into the bin. Newsletters or journals that you receive, if you did not request them and they are not central to the performance of your job, can also go into the bin. We offer this advice at the risk of it, being redundant, for our years of experience have shown us that much of what is lying on clients' desks is often unsolicited mail and journals that ideally will be read 'one of these days'. Re-engineer your decision-making process about what to keep so you are not holding onto everything that arrives, only the important information.

■ Active or non-active storage

When you receive information it will be in the following forms: paper letters, memos or reports, faxes, electronic documents, e-mail, voice mail, pages or telephone contacts. Essentially one good principle to use to organise your electronic or paper information is to keep it in the same format in which it arrived. For instance, if you receive a report via fax or in a paper format and you need to read it and then retain it, put it in a paper file. If you receive a document on a diskette from a co-worker who wants you to look at the document and make any needed changes, keep that information on the diskette. The one exception to this strategy is if you have decided that you want an electronic office. Then paper information will be scanned into your PC.

Voice information is different. Much of the information we receive through voice mail, phone discussions or pagers will be remembered and will not be recorded in the computer or on paper. This is especially true for information received from a pager. Usually you will return that call quickly and not need to store any information or phone numbers on your pager. Voice mail should only be used to store information for a short time. If you are busy, or out of town and unable to return all phone calls immediately, storing your phone messages on your voice mail system for a short time can be a good idea.

These principles also apply to miscellaneous information, such as business cards or spoken information that you want to make sure you remember. Essentially the same rule applies. If you have a business card you want to keep, this should go in the same place as your other business cards.

In all of this you are following the same model as a manufacturing plant. When you receive information you need to read it or act on it and then put it in its place. When you buy groceries, you bring them home and put them in the appropriate place. When a manufacturing plant receives its raw materials or parts, they go into the specific area where they belong. This way time is not wasted in looking for essential materials. This is why it is crucial to set up a PIM strategy that identifies what files you need and where they are. When working with our clients we have seen how easily they have run into problems when they do not have appropriate files, whether it is directories on the computer or paper files. When they receive new information, they have no other option than to put the paper on top of their desk as no file exists where it can go.

In the absence of a good filing system, either computer or paper, it is as if you have taken ten different puzzles and mixed all the pieces together. Then you begin to put each individual puzzle together, working on more than one at a time. No wonder we do not have enough hours in the day!

CHAPTER 12

Computing technology and your personal information management strategy

While they may look more organised than a pile of papers or a bulging file, software and its accompanying hardware tools still have the capacity to move towards chaos quickly. One of the reasons for this is that, even though the number of software programs and files is increasing rapidly, the physical size of the computer does not increase. Also the computer looks exactly the same whether you have 10 or ten or 10 000 files stored.

It is essential to include software in your PIM strategy. The information contained in software and hardware must be organised and sorted through just as closely as you did with your paper files. Careful attention must be paid to periodically purging the computer files that you are no longer using and no longer have a need to save. Computer files should be subject to the same criteria that were established for your paper files. If you decided you did not need to keep project files more than a year after they were completed, why keep the computer files?

Software, while an excellent tool to manage information, cannot do the job by itself. For example, a company may have expense reports forms on a computer network, instead of handing out paper forms. Even though the report can be generated on the computer, the paper receipts must be hooked up with the expense form and turned in. Another situation where this occurs is with bookkeeping or financial software. While these programs can automate and speed up the process of producing financial reports and paying bills, there is no escaping retaining the paper-based invoices and receipts that go along with the expenditure.

Once the document is created, the user has an information management question to answer. Should the document be stored by printing a copy and putting it in the filing cabinet, or should it be stored in the computer? Typically what happens is that the document is stored in both the computer software program and on paper in the filing cabinet. This duplication for hundreds of documents increases the amount of filing space needed and uses up the computer's hard disk storage capacity. You would not store two copies of the same thing in the same file, so why have two copies in two places?

Storing the document in the computer has several benefits. The document can be located easily: most word processors have quick and powerful search facilities that allow you to locate documents using a key word. If your file structure is not the clearest, or you cannot remember where you stored something, this option will save time. A search of 200 documents on the computer can be done in a matter of seconds. Compare that to searching through the equivalent number of papers or files. Or worse, if a paper document is misfiled in a client's file, imagine trying to track that down. If it is misfiled in the wrong computer directory the computer can locate it within seconds by doing a search of the entire directory.

■ How to manage information in the computer

While we have talked about organising papers at some length, this chapter will discuss managing electronic information. Although the mediums are very different, the concepts behind the management of the information are the same. The first thing you must do is determine what your important categories of information are, just as you did with your papers. Instead of setting up a file for each category, you would set up a directory, which is similar to a filing drawer. Within the directory, you can have sub-categories of information, as well as individual pieces of information. For instance, you may know you need a directory for *clients*. Underneath a *client* directory, you can create a directory using the client's *name* or *company name*. Within each directory, you could further divide it into categories such as *proposals, memos, marketing, billing* or anything else that is appropriate.

The point to setting up directories is to identify where information is likely to be so that it can be accessed quickly. For example, for one client you may have two sub-directories, one for marketing before the client signed on, and one for memos, which are inter-office memos that have been written to co-workers. Inside the directory will be a series of correspondence and proposals going to the client:

Directory: *Clients*
   Sub-Directory: *Adams*
      Sub-Directory: *Marketing*
      Sub-Directory: *Memos*
            Letter.01
            Letter.02
            Publicity
            Jones
      Sub-Directory: *Plan*

Using MSDOS, the file 'path name' would look like this:

C:\msword\msdocs\clients\adams\marketing\plan.

Plan is the marketing document located in the *Adams* client sub-directory in your word processing program. (The examples we will use here are from the text-based system MSDOS, but the same general principles apply to the graphical user interfaces or GUIs, discussed in earlier chapters. Even though GUIs provide a visual environment for the user, where files and folders are represented by small visual icons, the ways in which they can be structured are the same.)

Continuing with the MSDOS example, after you have installed your word processing program, it is helpful to create a directory called *msdocs* or *docs*. In this directory, all of the word processing documents you create will be located here. These should be separate from the program files so you do not get involved with searching through them to look for data files. Also, if you need to examine program files for any reason, it is easier to look at them if the data files are not mixed in with them.

The names on the files can be as specific or general as needed. *Jones.04* indicates that the letter is about someone named *Jones* and it is the fourth document. *Publicity* is the subject of the letter. Sometimes people remember documents according to when they were written. *Letter.02* indicates it is a letter, and the number indicates whether it was the last one written. That information, accompanied by the date, is often sufficient for people to find the documents again. In order to define more clearly what a file is about, extensions can be used. Typically, the file name is eight characters long, followed by a three character extension. The extension can indicate the type of document such as *let* (letter), *mem* (memo) or a combination of letters and numbers, *lt6* (letter number six). (While Microsoft's Windows95 gives you additional options, for those people still using DOS and Windows-based programs, this system will still apply.)

These guidelines are appropriate to software programs such as word processing packages and spreadsheets. They allow you to enter many different kinds of information and create the structure of your document. However, for other software programs, such as calendars, databases and personal organisers, information is entered and then retrieved without naming the file. For instance, a calendar package contains information about your appointments. If you want to know when next month's conference is precisely, you just look at that month's page and your eyes will focus on the information. The only recall operation you have to do is to remember what software package the information is in. To find a telephone number of someone in your databases, you perform a search command on that person's name. No other retrieval system is required.

■ Word processing information storage tips

Beyond the ability to find documents quickly, there are other ways a word processing package can be useful to help you manage information. While effective, some of these techniques may not be commonly suggested by the software package.

□ Forms

Word processing forms that need to be used repeatedly can be stored in a directory by themselves. Within that directory, the names of the forms can indicate their use. Then the forms can be saved in a 'read-only' format. This may be a standard form letter, such as a marketing letter. Basically this is any information that you routinely send out, with only minor modifications.

□ Envelope forms

Envelopes that are used repeatedly, such as monthly bills, clients' names, or monthly accounts payable can be stored in a directory called *envelopes*. They can be stored by using the last name, or the name of the company. Instead of entering the key strokes each time an envelope needs to be sent, a print command can be given and the envelope produced within a few seconds.

While these ideas may not be the most traditional ones for storage of information, they have certain benefits. First, they require no additional software program or the learning curve that would go with it. Second, the data entered in this manner will seamlessly co-ordinate with your word processing program. There will be no problems in getting one file to read the other.

■ Client listing and addresses

While the standard answer to storing and managing information such as addresses and telephone and fax numbers is to put it into a database, some information can also be put into a word processing package. If you intend to do a lot of mailings it can be saved in a 'merge format'. This way the information can be merged into mailing labels or into a form letter.

One client, a journalist, decided this was how he wanted to keep track of the names, numbers and addresses of his sources, which were numerous. Some were called frequently, others less frequently. He grouped the sources according to the subject matter he would call them about. This worked well, as about half of each category of people he called infrequently and he probably would not remember their specific company or name. However, if he had them listed as government sources, he could pick anyone randomly from this list. He already had the word processing package and knew how to use it. Furthermore, he was already in the package and could quickly switch to another screen to take notes once the person answered. Changes to the names and numbers could be made quickly and easily.

■ Information managers

If you are looking for additional assistance in finding files, and even have trouble remembering what software program the information might be in, there are other software programs that may be helpful, such as WordPerfect's *Information Central*.

While these programs are useful, the problem is not usually remembering what software package your information is in.

■ E-mail

E-mail is often best managed if it is left in the software program in clearly labelled filing cabinets or in-boxes. Because much of e-mail communication is informal, messages can easily be deleted as soon as they have been read, or within a few days. If you do need the information to be included in another document, e-mail messages can be imported into your word processing package, saving the time taken to retype it. Some packages, such as the excellent *Eudora* (for Macs and PCs) provide an extensive set of tools for structuring and searching directories and sub-directories of incoming, outgoing, discarded and filed mail.

■ Voice

Voice mail can be used as a short-term storage device for phone numbers of calls that need to be returned. This is particularly helpful if you are travelling and you do not want to carry another piece of paper in your wallet or personal organiser. This solution will work as long as those numbers are also contained in another area or database and the voice mail is not relied upon for permanent storage.

■ Maintenance

While information is stored on the computer, it still needs to be evaluated at least once every six or 12 months to make sure it is still relevant. Files that are several years old and are no longer required lose their value just as quickly as paper-based information.

▌Innovative computer-based personal information management strategies

■ A fully computerised solution

Using personal computers, professionals have a powerful tool at their disposal to assist them in completing their work. That power is especially helpful to the process of running a small business. Here is how one business owner uses his computer and one desk filing drawer to manage his computer consulting business employing five people and a £200 000 computer system.

- Letters to clients or other people, as well as proposals to clients, are filed within the word processing software. Letters for new business are contained in the business directory. Letters and notes for each client are contained in a directory for each client, which is a sub-directory of the client directory. An envelope directory contains envelopes for clients and others who are frequently sent letters. *WinFax*, a fax program that allows faxing directly from the computer without printing, is also used to create a paperless operation.

- Billing is accomplished by entering time entries at the end of each day into the software package. As employees turn in their weekly time sheets, the information is entered. Invoices for purchased materials for clients are also entered as they are received during the month, and copies of the invoice are produced and sent out. As the billing is handled each day, this prevents the task from piling up and allows the time entries to be made when everything is still fresh in the mind. Envelopes for the invoices are printed from the word processing software.
- To manage finances, an accounting package is used that prints cheques and automatically produces accounting reports according to the expense category selected. Monthly reports show instantly what the financial situation of the company is.
- Names and telephone numbers of contacts and clients are included in a database, and a file listing is printed to make using the information as simple as possible.

■ Mobile computing solutions

One solution to information management using computers is to adopt a fully mobile solution. Many of the PDA devices we discussed earlier, in addition to slightly larger 'notebook' or 'subnotebook' computers (computers with all the power of a desk-based PC, but smaller), are being used. Here users upload information they require for, say, a business trip along with software for communications. This means that they are free to work on important projects wherever they are. However this solution is still fraught with difficulties, of which we have personal experience: consider this diary entry by one of us on a business trip to the USA:

Sunday: Leave Heathrow for a week in the US, attending a computing conference in Nashville, then travelling on to Chicago via a meeting at MIT's Media Lab. in Boston. I have, as usual, brought a laptop with me, and this time ensured I have a variety of power cables to cope with any possible eventuality. Usually I lug a computer half-way round the world and arrive somewhere to find I can't plug it in. This trip I am also reading and sending e-mail via a CompuServe account to keep in touch with my office, so I have also brought a selection of telephone cables to make sure I can surf the information superhighway with ease. Ironic that my £3000 computer can only interconnect to the world's most sophisticated telephone system and several million user global computer network with a £2.00 bit of copper wire.

Monday: I plug into the hotel phone system to pick up e-mail. For some inexplicable reason, I can't connect to the local access CompuServe number. All this is terribly reminiscent of previous trips and the usual fiascos with power cables. Having tried all alternatives I use the knife from breakfast to slice open the phone cable and start splicing wires together. This eventually works, and I now have a £3000 computer, connected to the world's most sophisticated telephone system and a several million user global computer network by a £2.00 bit of copper wire held together by sticking plaster. What better illustration of how the information superhighway isn't really accessible to everyone after all.

Wednesday: Arrive in Boston and check into my hotel relieved to find that I can dial into the local number to pick up mail with my improvised telephone cable. The irony that I am using this set-up to mail to a colleague at MIT, one of the places where the most advanced communication technology is being developed, is not lost on me. Mike Hawley, professor at MIT whom I am meeting, is amused by the cable saga. We talk about future systems in which people are freed from the constraints of cabled networks, and can wander round their environment wearing their computers which are connected via wireless links to other devices. The ability to not rely on cables is one of the key enablers for future computer communications systems as it has been with cellular telephones.

Friday: More meetings at MIT where we discuss Mike Hawley's work in the Personal Information Architecture Group at the Media Lab. Mike is interested in designing what he calls the BodyNet: a complete system for linking up computational devices – watches, clothes which have computational power, chairs which respond to the user's movements – with the 'bitstream' of information on the superhighway. One thing we are both interested in is how users can effectively access such devices, through mechanisms such as voice, sound, gesture and touch. The Media Lab is working on many different ways of allowing people to effectively access the bitstream of data flooding around us down copper wire, through optical cables, or via satellite broadcast. Nicholas Negroponte, director of the Media Lab whose book Being Digital *suggests that the 'digerati' – those people whose work is with the bits of information rather than the atoms of objects – require new kinds of tools: intelligent agents which can sort and act on information, or tools for 'pulling bits' out of the bitstream, rather than passively accepting bits 'pushed' from broadcasts, for example.*

Saturday: Arrive in Chicago, where I am meeting a colleague to work on a book on managing information [this book of course] *to be published later in the year. Reviewing my e-mail, I see that I have read and sent some 200 e-mail messages to colleagues from the UK, US and Europe over the last five days. I wonder what I used to do before this was possible. Waiting for me at the hotel is a* Federal Express *package from the UK containing some contracts to sign. The atoms of the contracts have been transported, at great cost, across the Atlantic only to have more atoms applied by me (the ink of a signature) and packaged in more atoms (an envelope) and the whole collection of atoms transported back across the Atlantic. Being digital clearly has its advantages.*

Here we can see that it may be the non-obvious problems (the wiring of telephone cables) which make mobile information management solutions a problem.

■ A personal information management strategy not using a computer

Although we have discussed using software and other technology that will help you manage your information, it is not mandatory to have a computer. It is possible to run a business using only papers. One client did just that. She is an image consultant with a successful business who did not want to spend the time and effort to get a computer and learn how to use it. She had no previous computer experience and her learning curve would have been significant.

One of the first things we did was determine what work needed to be done, and what was just for the active archives. The work that needed to be done we separated into two different categories. One was called *urgent* and contained things that needed to be done within a day or two. This went into a file pocket envelope and stayed at the side of her table. As she worked out of her home, this was a convenient way to keep all of her urgent 'to do' information together, yet allow the table to be used for other purposes when she was not working. The other file pocket envelope contained less urgent work, and could be done within the next week or so. Some of the items that were lying around were bills that needed to be paid. The client did not want to pay these each time one arrived. So we designated one spot where bills would be put until it was time to pay them.

Client invoices were organised. To keep things simple, all copies of client invoices went into one notebook. Then we developed a simple form that listed the invoices outstanding as well as other details. With about five minutes' work putting the month's invoices into the notebook and filling out the form listing the receivables, the consultant could now see what her cash flow situation was.

Paid bills were hole-punched into a separate notebook, at the front of which was a simple spreadsheet that held the expenses categories listed. As each cheque was paid, the amount was allocated to the appropriate category. Totalling the amount of cheques and the individual expenses categories at the end of the month provided a cross-checking mechanism that made sure no calculations were done incorrectly. Financial information is one thing that accounting software handles very easily. However, in the absence of time, money and motivation, doing your books yourself on paper accomplishes the task in the same way as the computer accomplishes it.

Next we took a look at what information was lying around. Much of it was resource information. Our image consultant would do seminars for her corporate clients. Each time she did a seminar, she would use a basic format, adding specifics for each company. To do this she would pull out lots of her resource information gleaned from seminars as well as books she had read. We went through this information, and she decided that half of it could be thrown away, as much of it was no longer useful. She realised that most of it was now information that was part of her own mental knowledge base. Some of the information was quite important. In some cases the important information was added to existing files and in other cases new files were created.

Then we looked at the existing files. The consultant went through each file and decided which she did not need. After about five minutes of looking at the files she made the remark that she had kept a lot of things that she did not need any more. While all of the information had been valuable and useful when it was originally saved, it was no longer valuable: she had already learned and assimilated what she needed to know and did not need to have the papers lying around any longer. After that realisation, she began tossing out the papers much more quickly. When she was finished, 75 per cent of her files were gone. Did she later regret throwing something away? The answer was no.

Worrying about throwing away something important is a fear that grips many people who are attempting to put order into their offices. However, out of all of the clients we have worked with, no one has been traumatised by throwing something away. In fact the rule of thumb is that, during every organisation operation, one thing (only one) out of the hundreds or thousands that are discarded will be missed. When that happens, the reaction usually is, 'I wish I had saved it, but I can get it elsewhere', or, 'While I wish I had saved it, the truth is I don't even think I really need it.'

CHAPTER 13
Conclusions

In the previous chapters we have looked at:

- the problems of the information age;
- the concept of information overload;
- information, why it is important and how it is used;
- personal information management products;
- developing and maintaining a PIM strategy;
- computers and your PIM strategy.

In this chapter we will look some of the ways that you can ensure that you continue to manage your personal information effectively, even in the face of problems you might encounter.

■ Technology and change

We started this book by saying that times change, but problems remain the same. One of the changes is in the development of technology, and to remain able to manage personal information effectively you will need to recognise the importance of changing technology. You will need to evaluate open-mindedly the possible benefits and uses of new technology. As history has shown time and time again, the failure to take seriously new developments has led to not seizing the best opportunity. Some of the following examples might show you what we mean (these appeared in a message broadcast on the Internet):

> This 'telephone' has too many shortcomings to be seriously considered as a means of communication. The device is inherently of no value to us. (Western Union internal memo, 1876)
> Who the hell wants to hear actors talk? (H.M. Warner, Warner Brothers, 1927)
> Heavier-than-air flying machines are impossible. (Lord Kelvin, president, Royal Society, 1895)
> So we went to Atari and said, 'Hey, we've got this amazing thing, even built with some of your parts, and what do you think about funding us? Or we'll give it to you. We just want to do it. Pay our salary, we'll come work for you.' And they said, 'No.' So then we went to Hewlett-Packard, and they said, 'Hey, we don't need you. You haven't got through college yet.' (Apple Computer Inc. founder Steve Jobs on attempts to get Atari and Hewlett-Packard interested in the idea of the 'personal computer')
> Drill for oil? You mean drill into the ground to try and find oil? You're crazy. (Drillers whom Edwin L. Drake tried to enlist for his project to drill for oil in 1859)

125

I think there's a world market for about five computers. (Thomas J. Watson, Chairman of the Board, IBM)
The bomb will never go off. I speak as an expert in explosives. (Admiral William Leahy, US Atomic Bomb Project)
Airplanes are interesting toys but of no military value. (Ferdinand Foch, Professor of Strategy, Ecole Supérieure de Guerre)
Man will never reach the moon regardless of all future scientific advances. (Lee DeForest, inventor of the vacuum tube and father of television)
Everything that can be invented has been invented. (Charles H. Duell, Commissioner, US Office of Patents, 1899)

Although these are intentionally humorous examples, it is clearly possible to under-estimate the possibilities of new developments. In the following section we will look briefly at some of the new technological developments which will have an enormous impact on the way information is manipulated and will affect your PIM strategy.

■ 'Techno trends'

In his book *Techno-Trends* (1994) Daniel Burrus looks at a number of ways in which you can 'use technology to help go beyond your competition'. One of the key elements that Burrus identifies is the link between *time* and *technology* which we have made in previous chapters. Burrus suggest that one of the most import-ant uses of technology is in fact to 'leverage' time – to make the most effective use of time. This is very important since, in contrast to the 1950s, when people were saying that new technology would increase our leisure time, we now have much less time owing to (amongst other things) the speed of communications. Technology means that most people actually do more, not less. It makes sense, then, to try and use technology in the ways which make the best use of a pre-cious resource – our time.

The next few paragraphs will identify several new technologies which we be-lieve will have a tremendous impact on the way information is managed.

■ Cellular communications and PCNs

One of the key technologies which will have a tremendous impact on all of us is the development of 'mobile communications' and, in particular, the growth of 'cellular digital communications'. 'Cellular' means that information is transferred over the air by a network of transmitters, each of which has a small coverage area or 'cell'. As you move around, the transmitters 'hand off' your mobile tele-phone conversation to each other as you move. This hand-off is of course in-visible to you, and your conversation carries on, even though a new cell is now handling it.

The cellular telephones we have today are mostly still based on what is known as 'analogue' technology. Although we will not provide a technical explanation of this, it effectively means that the signal has a very low 'bandwidth' (the amount of information that can be transmitted) and also has quite low quality (cellular telephone conversations are often punctuated by gaps, pauses and hisses). New 'digital' cellular technology provides not only higher bandwidth and better quality, but also is more reliable, allowing you to send computer data and faxes, as well as have conversations, using a mobile telephone. Even more sophisticated are new 'personal communications networks' (PCNs) which allow you to do things like sending short text messages to other telephones, or diverting calls to other telephones, pagers or fax machines.

For personal information management the impact will be enormous: you will now have another source of information (the airwaves) with information flooding at you not only in the office, but in your car, on the street or on the train. And it is likely that these networks will increase in sophistication until images – in the form of 'digital video' – can be transmitted. All of this with something you can hold in one hand! To learn the latest developments, the book *Using Wireless Communications in Business* by Andrew M. Seybold (1994) is a good start.

■ Portable and notebook computers

We have looked at computer hardware and software, but the largest growth in computing technology is in the development of small and portable computers. These go by various names: 'laptop', 'portable', 'notebook', 'sub-notebook', 'palmtop' and, as we discussed earlier, the 'personal digital assistant' or PDA. These terms indicate a decrease in size from 'laptop' (the largest portable computer) to PDA (the smallest, currently).

As with the mobile telephone, the development of small computers which have almost the power of a desktop PC, with many megabytes of storage, colour displays and facilities for connecting to a modem (either a fixed telephone modem of a cellular modem), will change the ways we manage information. The trend is that computers will become smaller and even more powerful, and will do more of the things that desktop computers can currently do.

■ Multimedia

A further development is what is known as 'multimedia' technology. 'Multimedia', as the name suggests, means that computers can store, manipulate and display information in various forms – not only text, but images and sounds. Computers that are designed for multimedia require a large amount of storage and a lot of computing power, which is needed if, for example, you want to look at a database of film clips which will allow you to see excerpts from a movie, read its script and listen to the soundtrack.

Again, multimedia is another form of information you will need to manage, and manage effectively.

■ Intelligent agents

Finally, in the more distant future, some of our information on computers will be managed by what are being called 'intelligent agents'. The idea of intelligent computers has been around for some time – often in science fiction (remember HAL, the intelligent computer in the film '2001: A Space Odyssey'?) – but computers which can do *some* things intelligently (if not actually think like a human) are becoming a reality.

'Intelligent agents' are small software programs which can help you out by, for example, filtering your e-mail messages (looking for the names of people who sent the messages), keeping track of your diary appointments (checking for confusions or clashes, or reminding you that you have a meeting) or looking for information on a computer network.

The prediction is that all computers will some day have an intelligent agent, helping you to manage your information more effectively.

■ Predicting technologies

Of course, it is all very well saying, 'Look for the best new technologies which can save you time and then use them', but it is difficult for most people to see how technologies will develop. As we saw at the opening of the chapter, predictions can be *very* wide of the mark.

The second insight provided in Burrus' *Techno-Trends* is about the way technologies develop, and how they can be used at various stages of their development. Burrus suggests that technologies have a 'life cycle' which is pretty much the same for all technologies. This allows us to see how attributes such as their cost, availability on the market, the risks of using them and their value to their users are related to one another. Figure 13.1 suggests that technologies which can be classed as 'future' – still on the drawing board – and not available on the market, are of a potentially low value, of high cost and extremely high risk. As technologies 'emerge' and become 'available' the cost and the risk of using them declines, and their availability and value increases. Then, as technologies move towards 'obsolescence', their cost (but also their value) decline but their availability increases.

There are many examples of this life cycle, but perhaps one of the most obvious is telecommunications, and particularly new forms of mobile communication we have discussed. As cellular telephones were developed they were very expensive and not really available to most people. As telephone handsets became more widely used, their cost declined and their value increased, and they could be purchased in many high street stores. However analogue cellular telephones are now in the 'applied' phase, and will soon decline into obsolescence, partly because of the development of digital cellular telephones, which are in the emerging phase of the life cycle. The development of the PCNs we have talked about will eventually push analogue cellular telephones into obsolescence, where they will become (like gramophones, for example) collectors' items with little practical value.

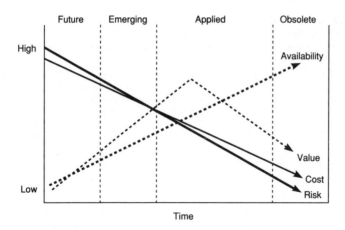

Figure 13.1 Technology life cycles.

Source: Adapted from Burrus (1994).

One of the implications of the technology life cycle is that, in order to use technology effectively, one must make the most of technologies in their 'applied' phase, and pay attention to new technologies which replace them. Adopting a new technology *early* in its 'applied' phase will mean paying more, but also means that you will get the longest possible useful life from it. Adopting technologies *late* in the 'applied' phase will mean that they are cheaper, but there will be less useful life. In the example of cellular telephones (at least in Europe) those adopting analogue cellular telephones will soon realise that new emerging digital services are of higher value, even though they are of higher cost.

All of this is of course complicated by the fact that the technological pace of change is increasingly rapid: whereas television took something like 30 years from invention to full development, the transistor – which is the basis for modern computing – took only ten years. It is likely that, for sophisticated computing and communications, the time from invention to development and then to application will be even shorter.

■ Preventing information build-up

Although we will summarise the major points for easy reference at the end of the book, we can make some very general concluding points which it will be useful to remember:

- Information management and organisation require *discipline*.
- There is a difference between *information* and *non-information*: non-information is so called because in the length of time it has been stored it has lost its value.

- Managing personal information is like a *puzzle*. When everything is in its place and fits, you have a pleasant picture that makes a great deal of sense. If everything is randomly tossed about, you have no picture and a hunting expedition to find what you need.
- Having a PIM strategy is like having many roads to travel down and a thorough map to guide your way, along with knowledge of where you are going. Contrast that with having many roads to take, no decision about where you want to go, and no map to guide you.
- Less information means *more clarity*. The fewer items you have to look through, the easier it will be to remember and find what you need. You will also be able to reduce the amount of structure that you need to build into your information retrieval system.

One problem our clients typically encounter in managing their personal information, being organised and believing they do not have enough time is that they fail to break large projects into smaller pieces. What is more beneficial is to separate the entire task into small, 'bite-sized' pieces that can be accomplished during an available 15 or 30 minutes. If you wait for a day with nothing on the calendar, you may be waiting for a long time.

If you have a big project such as writing a 20-page proposal, this can be broken down into two categories: 'thinking activities' and 'doing activities'. Thinking activities are those that require uninterrupted quiet time. Doing activities do not require uninterrupted quiet time and they can be scheduled during smaller, available chunks of time. Here is how this situation works. You have been assigned a 20-page proposal to complete for a potential client. You have two weeks in which to prepare it. This is plenty of time, unless you leave the task to the very last minute. To begin this project, you first focus on thinking activities, which need non-interruptible time. The first thing you do is outline and plan the report. This will take approximately 30 minutes. After this stage is complete, you do other work and take phone calls. Next you begin to write the text of the report, breaking the writing into several sections. You write only one or two sections at one sitting. These writing sessions will take place over several days. Then you schedule one to two hours to edit the report.

After you have a solid draft, you switch to the 'doing activities'. First you show the report to your boss and spend 10 minutes talking to him. This can be done during a busy day when you can squeeze in this conversation between other phone calls and appointments. The suggested changes are minor and do not cause any major changes. You find the time to make the changes one at a time. The editing changes are accomplished over a two-day period. After the changes are made, you read the report in its entirety, looking for poor sentences or bad wording. As you know what it says, this is approached as a doing activity.

The next day you schedule an uninterrupted hour to look at the report once more. As it looks good, you give it to your PA to make some minor changes and adjust the formatting. When the report is given back to you, you switch into doing activity. You look at the report to proofread it and to make sure that all of the required changes were made. You do this as you take phone calls and people come into your office.

To keep all of the report papers organised easily, you have put everything in one folder as you finished working on each stage of the project. As you want to begin work on the report during the next day, you move your other papers to one side of your desk and bring out the papers from the folder. This prevents wasting time hunting for missing pages or notes, but, most importantly, as you make changes to the text, using your word processing program, you discard the paper copies where you had indicated changes by hand.

While your work may entail something other than writing a report, the principles remain the same. Often when people become overwhelmed by large or difficult projects they tend to let things pile up, causing crises and wasting time searching for what is needed. Breaking projects into manageable pieces guarantees that they will be completed successfully.

■ Some real problems

For some people who are experiencing extreme difficulties and emotional distress in trying to organise and eliminate their excessive amounts of paper, there may be a deeper cause. Sometimes personal information management problems are caused by psychological problems, rather than just poor business and efficiency habits.

The *Diagnostic and Statistical Manual of Mental Disorders* (DSM-IV) lists eight diagnostic criteria for 'Obsessive–Compulsive Personality Disorder', and says that diagnosis is indicated by the presence of four of the eight criteria. The criterion directly related to organisation is 'unable to discard worn-out or worthless objects even when they have no sentimental value'. Throwing these items out is seen as wasteful, and sufferers may become angry if someone else attempts to dispose of them. The problem is extreme if the person's family members or roommates complain about the number of items lying around, or when papers or other items are stacked so high that they present a fire hazard or it is difficult to walk through a room. Studies cited in the DSM-IV suggest that the prevalence of Obsessive–Compulsive Personality Disorder (OCPD) occurs in about 1 per cent of the community, and in about 3–10 per cent of individuals who go to mental health clinics in the USA (American Psychiatric Association, 1994, pp.670–71).

A research study by Frost and Gross suggested that perhaps indecisiveness is the more basic problem and hoarding is simply a manifestation of it. Deciding what to keep or to throw away may be so difficult for 'hoarders' that they continually postpone the decision or they make the 'safe' decision to keep everything (Frost and Gross, 1993, p.372). In another aspect of their study, over 100 items were listed by self-identified hoarders as the target of their saving. The study showed that:

81% of the subjects saved clothes;
50% saved magazines;
43% saved bags;
40% saved books;

37% saved school papers;
31% saved cards/letters.

Also 61 per cent of the people in the study said that they engaged in hoarding behaviour at work as well as at home.

Frost and Gross also asked the subjects what altered their hoarding behaviour. Most frequently cited was 'moving house'; also cited was 'running out of room'. And, with the advent of recycling programmes, many people found they could recycle papers, while they had been unable to throw them away (Frost and Gross, 1993, pp.373–4). Asked about what age their behaviour began, 66 per cent of the hoarders said that it started during childhood and 25 per cent said that it started during their teens or early 20s.

From what we have seen working with clients, it is not surprising that moving house triggers a change. Moving is a task that no one looks forward to, even with the assistance of professional movers, so it is not surprising that packing, moving, unpacking and then putting away quickly brings a sobering realisation that many of the papers and possessions that were being packed were hardly worth it. Even when we ask our clients to go through their accumulated papers by looking at each one individually, they are hard pressed to state a logical reason (even to themselves) for needing certain papers. After this realisation, paper can often go into the bin.

Another psychological problem that has an impact upon being organised and managing information is 'Attention Deficit Disorder' (ADD). 'Attention Deficit/ Hyperactivity Disorder, Predominantly Inattentive Type' is indicated if six or more of the listed ten criteria are met for six months or longer. Three of the criteria that directly relate to personal information management are:

1. often has difficulty organising tasks and activities;
2. often loses things necessary for tasks or activities; and
3. is often easily distracted by extraneous stimuli. (American Psychiatric Association, 1994, p.84)

These syndromes are discussed in order to give you information about certain situations where professional psychological help may be necessary. However, just because you do not want to get rid of unnecessary items, hate the idea of weeding through your papers and would definitely rather be doing something else, this does not mean that you need professional help. Many people do not like organising their information, sorting through everything and throwing things away. Just because the process is uncomfortable, this does not mean you have a disorder!

■ Summary

Everything in this book has been written to help you to manage your information effectively and to become more efficient and organised. If you see an idea or concept that makes sense to you, use it. If something does not make any sense or does not seem to apply to your situation, please disregard it.

While managing your personal information and being organised do not have to be difficult, the path to managing your personal information effectively is not always trouble-free. E-mail that does not mail and faxes that do not fax are time-consuming problems. Your own attitudes and mind set also have a part to play. If you procrastinate, or are feeling overwhelmed, you will be unable to work effectively. How do you cope with these problems? Look at Figure 13.2 and circle those problems which are preventing you from managing your information and being effective. You may need to circle all, a few, or have others to add. When you have identified the problems you can begin tackling them, one at a time. Remember, the idea is not to change your habits overnight but to try for small and gradual improvements.

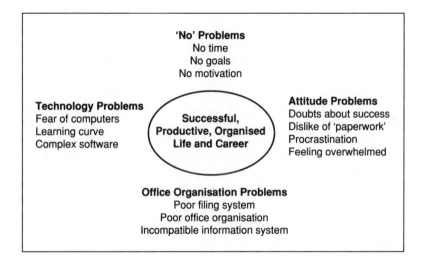

Figure 13.2   Problems that affect a successful, productive and organised life and career

■ Guarantee for successful information management

To summarise our recommendations, here is a guarantee for successful information management:

- Know what you must keep and eliminate the rest.
- Information is perishable. The garbage can accumulate either in your office or in the landfill. Which do you prefer?
- Too much information becomes disinformation. Retain your information carefully.

- Complete your tasks. Non-completion is often the major cause of poor information management.

In addition to these tips, you also need the appropriate mind set:

- You have to want to do it.
- You have to focus on it.
- You have to set some time aside.
- You have to have a strategy.
- You have to practise.

Only then will you be successful in managing your information and your possessions.

Appendix 1: key issues in personal information management

■ General principles

Define what information is important
Be cautious about what you save
Have a system for what you save and where you put it
Use your brain more effectively
Manage information technology

■ 'Information re-engineering goals and benefits

Make your information more accessible
Streamline the way you deal with information
Remove 'islands' of information
Reduce your information overload
Improve your personal effectiveness
Improve the effectiveness of your team or colleagues
Increase your satisfaction or 'congruence'

■ Eight key information actions

Create
Change
Store
Retrieve
Receive
Make decisions
Communicate
Discard

■ Five 'technology potentials'

Flow
Breadth
Depth
Accessibility
Interconnectedness

■ How to make using a computer easier

You *can* learn how to use the computer
Establish a plan for learning to use the computer
Purchase software from the same company

▌ Producing and implementing your own personal information management strategy

Your PIM strategy is derived from your goals
Information is perishable
The importance of information decreases with time

■ Benefits of a PIM strategy

Stress
Being overwhelmed
Time saving
Efficiency

■ Roadblocks to effective personal information management

Procrastination
Problems or situations that seem overwhelming
Too many organisational information systems
Business growing rapidly
Unusual circumstances
Paperwork
Denial and avoidance
Where to start
Lack of self-confidence
The 'pack-rat' syndrome

Appendix 2: personal information management products

Below are listed many of the most popular software applications for personal information management, including some we have discussed in the book. We do not endorse any of these products. There are, however, hundreds more, and new applications are constantly appearing. Details of these, with analyses and reviews, can be found in many of the personal computing magazines available in the UK and USA.

■ Spreadsheets

□ Quattro Pro

USA
WordPerfect Novell Applications Group
1555 N. Technology Way
Orem, UT 84057-2399
1-800-526-5203

UK
Novell UK
Novell House
London Road
Bracknell
Berkshire
RG12 2UY
01344 724000

□ Lotus 123

USA
Lotus Development Corporation
55 Cambridge Parkway
Cambridge, MA 02142
617-577-8500

UK
Lotus Development
Lotus Park
The Causeway
Staines
Middlesex
TW18 3AG
01784 455445

□ Microsoft Excel

USA
Microsoft Corporation
One Microsoft Way
Redmond, WA 98052
206-882-8080

UK
Microsoft Ltd
Microsoft Place
Winnersh Triangle
Wokingham
Berkshire
RG11 5TP
01734 270001

■ Finance/accounting packages

□ DacEasy, Inc

17950 Preston Road
Suite 800
Dallas, Texas 75252
1-800-Dac-Easy

□ Quickbooks and Quicken

Intuit, Inc.
P.O. Box 28815
Tucson, AZ 85775-2612
520-573-3699

□ M.Y.O.B. Accounting

Peachtree Accounting and Peachtree First Accounting
Subsidiary of Automatic Data Processing
1505 Pavilion Place
Norcross, GA 30093
404-564-5700

■ Billing software

□ Timeslips Corporation

17950 Preston Road
Suite 800
Dallas, Texas 75252
1-800-713-7479

■ Word processing

□ Lotus Ami Pro

USA
Lotus Development Corporation
55 Cambridge Parkway
Cambridge, MA 02142
617-577-8500

UK
Lotus Development
Lotus Park
The Causeway
Staines
Middlesex
TW18 3AG
01784 455445

□ WordPerfect

USA
WordPerfect Novell Applications Group
1555 N. Technology Way
Orem, UT 84057-2399
1-800-526-5203

UK
Novell UK
Novell House
London Road
Bracknell
Berkshire
RG12 2UY
01344 724000

□ Microsoft Word

USA
Microsoft Corporation
One Microsoft Way
Redmond, WA 98052
206-882-8080

UK
Microsoft Ltd
Microsoft Place
Winnersh Triangle
Wokingham
Berkshire
RG11 5TP
01734 270001

■ Database software
□ Lotus Organizer

USA
Lotus Development Corporation
55 Cambridge Parkway
Cambridge, MA 02142
617-577-8500

UK
Lotus Development
Lotus Park
The Causeway
Staines
Middlesex
TW18 3AG
01784 455445

□ Symantec's Act

USA
Symantec Corporation
10201 Torre Avenue
Cupertino, CA 95014
408-253-9600

UK
Symantec Ltd
St Cloud Gate
St Cloud Way
Maidenhead
Berkshire
SL6 8AW
01628 592222

□ SideKick

Philippe Kahn
Starfish Software
245M Mt. Hermon Road
Suite 313
Scotts Valley, CA 95066
1-800-370-8963

□ PackRat

Polaris Software
1928 Don Lee Place
Escondido, CA 92029
1-800-PACKRAT

□ Instant Recall

Chronologic Corporation
5151 N. Oracle #210
Tucson, AZ 85704
1-800-848-4970
602-293-3100

□ Microsoft Access, FoxPro

USA
Microsoft Corporation
One Microsoft Way
Redmond, WA 98052
206-832-8080

UK
Microsoft Ltd
Microsoft Place
Winnersh Triangle
Wokingham
Berkshire
RG11 5TP
01734 270001

□ Lotus Approach

USA
Lotus Development Corporation
55 Cambridge Parkway
Cambridge, MA 02142
1-800-343-5414

UK
Lotus Development
Lotus Park
The Causeway
Staines
Middlesex
TW18 3AG
01784 455445

☐ dBase, Paradox

USA
Borland
100 Borland Way
Scotts Valley, CA 95066
1-800-233-2444

UK
Borland UK
Ruscombe Business Park
Twyford
Berkshire
01734 321150

■ Personal organiser software
☐ 1stACT!

USA
Symantec Corporation
10201 Torre Avenue
Cupertino, CA 95014
408-253-9600

UK
Symantec Ltd
St Cloud Gate
St Cloud Way
Maidenhead
Berkshire
SL6 8AW
01628 592222

☐ NOW Contact

NOW Software Europe
1 Leighton Road
Heath and Reach
Bedfordshire
LU7 0AA
01525 237100

□ Borland SideKick

USA
Borland
100 Borland Way
Scotts Valley, CA 95066
1-800-233-2444

UK
Borland UK
Ruscombe Business Park
Twyford
Berkshire
01734 321150

□ Day-Timer Organizer

Day-Timers, Inc.
2855 Campus Drive
San Mateo, CA 94403
1-800-859-6955

□ Instant Recall

Chronologic Corporation
5151 N. Oracle #210
Tucson, AZ 85704
1-800-848-4970

□ Ascend

USA
Franklin Quest Company
2550 S. Decker Lake Blvd.
Salt Lake City, UT 84119
801-975-9992

UK
Mr Charles McAdam
31–33 Brunel Close
Drayton Fields Business Park
Daventry
NN11 5RB
01327 301311

■ Personal organiser paper systems

□ Time Manager International

USA
TMI North America
33 New Montgomery Street
Suite 310
San Francisco
CA 94105
415-957-1133

UK
TMI
50 High Street
Henley-in-Arden
Solihull
West Midlands
B95 5AN
01564 794100

□ Priority Manager International

USA
Day Runner, Inc.
2750 Moone Avenue
Fullerton, CA 92633
714-680-3500

UK
Day Runner Int.
Oxford House
15–17 Mt Ephraim Road
Tunbridge Wells
Kent
TN1 1EN
01892 516363

■ E-mail packages

□ Lotus Notes

USA
Lotus Development Corporation
55 Cambridge Parkway
Cambridge, MA 02142
617-577-8500

UK
Lotus Development
Lotus Park
The Causeway
Staines
Middlesex
TW18 3AG
01784 455445

□ Delphi

USA
Delphi International Services Corporation
620 Avenue of the Americas
18th St 5th Ave
6th Floor
NY10011
212-462-5000/6000

UK
Delphi Internet
The Elephant House
Hawley Crescent
London
NW1 8NP
0171 757 7080

■ Personal digital assistants
□ Apple's Newton

USA
Apple Computer Inc.,
Cupertino,
CA
800-770-4852

UK
Apple Computers UK Ltd
6 Roundwood Avenue
Stockley Park
Uxbridge
Middx
UB11 1BB
0181 569 1199

□ Psion Series 3

USA
Psion
150 Bakers Avenue
Conbord
MA 01742
508-371-0310

UK
Psion
85 Frampton Street
London
NW8
0171 262 5580

□ Sharp Zaurus

USA
Sharp Electronics Corp
1-800-BE-SHARP

UK
Sharp Commputers
84 Lily Road
London
SW6
0171 381 2553

□ Sony Magic Link

USA
Sony Electronics Inc
1 Sony Drive
Park Ridge
New Jersey 07656
201-930-1000

UK
Sony Electronics
Biabless Industrial Estate
Basingstoke
Hants
RD22 4SB
01256 55011

References

Preface

S. Lubar (1993) *Infoculture: The Smithsonian Book of Information Age Inventions* (Boston, Mass.: Houghton Mifflin) pp.37–172.

Chapter 1

D. Booher, (1986) *Cutting Paperwork in the Corporate Culture* (New York: Facts on File Publications) p.105.

J.S. Hirsch (1991) 'Flood of Information Swamps Managers, But some Are Finding Ways to Bail Out', *Wall Street Journal*, 12 August, page B1.

E. Lupton (1993) *Mechanical Brides* (New York: Cooper-Hewitt National Museum of Design, Smithsonian Institution) pp.45–7.

N. Negroponte (1995) *Being Digital* (New York: Alfred A. Knopf) p.89.

R.R. Panko (1985) 'Productivity Trends in Certain Office-Intensive Sectors of the U.S. Federal Government', *ACM Transactions on Office Information Systems*, vol. 3, no. 4, October pp. 370–79.

The Old Farmers Almanac (1978) Dublin, NH 03444.

'What happened to the paperless office?' (1994), *Association Management*, February, vol. 46, no. 2, p. 24.

Chapter 2

D. Booher (1986) *Cutting Paperwork in the Corporate Culture* (New York: Facts on File Publications) p.104.

A. Brown (1995) 'Paperwork is Target of Government's War on Waste', *Press Association News*, 31 July.

T. Buzan (1984) *Make the Most of Your Mind* (New York: Simon & Schuster) p.13.

Grolier Electronic Publishing (1995) *Grolier's Academic American Encyclopaedia*.

H.J. Heijn (1982) 'Automate the organization ... or organize the automation?', *Productivity Brief 14*, American Productivity Center, Houston, Texas, p.5.

W.O. Maedke, Mary F. Robek and Gerald F. Brown (1981) *Information and Records Management* (Encino, California: Glencoe).

Paperwork Relief' (1995) *Industry Week*, vol. 244, no. 12, p.71, 19 June.

I. Place and E.L. Popham (1966) *Filing and Records Management* (Englewood Cliffs, NJ: Prentice-Hall). p.9.

D.G. Rayner (1975) 'A battle won in the war on the paper bureaucracy', *Harvard Business Review*, January–February, pp.8–14.

W.J. Ridge (1969) *Value Analysis for Better Management* (Kingsport, Tennessee: The American Management Association).

I. Sinclair (1988) *Filofax Facts* (London: David Fulton) pp.1–5.

■ Chapter 4

S. Covey (1989) *The 7 Habits of Highly Effective People* (New York: Simon & Schuster).
E. DeBono (1985) *Edward de Bono's Masterthinker's Handbook: a Guide to Innovative Thinking* (London: Penguin).
M. Hammer and J. Champey (1994) *Re-engineering the Corporation* (New York: HarperCollins).
C. Livesay (1994) *Getting and Staying Organised* (New York: Irwin Professional Publishing).
J. Rhodes (1991) *Conceptual Toolmaking* (Oxford: Basil Blackwell).
A. Robbins (1988) *Unlimited Power* (London: Simon & Schuster, 1988).

■ Chapter 5

Investors Business Daily, 16 August 1995.

■ Chapter 6

R. Henkoff (1991) 'Make Your Office More Productive', *Fortune*, 25 February, p.73.)
P. Strassman (1985) *Information Payoff* (New York: The Free Press).

■ Chapter 7

N. Negroponte (1995) *Being Digital*, (New York: Alfred A. Knopf).
D.A. Norman (1993) *Things That Make Us Smart* (Reading, Mass.: Addison-Wesley) p.79.

■ Chapter 8

K. Alesandrini (1992) *Surviving Information Overload* (Homewood, Ill.: Business One Irwin) pp.8–9.
K. Aschner (ed.) (1983) *Taking Control of Your Office Records: A Manager's Guide* (White Plain, NY: Knowledge Industry Publications).

■ Chapter 9

K. Alesandrini (1992) *Surviving Information Overload* (Homewood, Ill.: Business One Irwin) pp.8–9.
L. Carroll (1984) *Alice in Wonderland* (New York: Alfred A. Knopf), pp.89–90; first published 1866 by Macmillan and Company.
L.W. Warren and J.C. Ostrom (1988) 'Pack Rats: World-Class Savers', *Psychology Today*, February, pp.58–62.

■ Chapter 10

I. Cole (1982) 'Human Aspects of Office Filing: Implications of the Electronic Office', *Proceedings of the Human Factors Society, the 26th Annual Meeting*, pp.59–68.
T.W. Malone (1983) 'How Do People Organize Their Desks? Implications for the Design of Office Information Systems', *ACM Transactions on Office Information Systems*, vol. 1, no. 1, January pp.99–112.
P. Russell (1979) *The Brain Book* (New York: Penguin Books) p.7.

■ Chapter 11

D.A. Norman (1993) *Things That Make Us Smart* (Reading, Mass.: Addison-Wesley) p.72.
D.G. Rayner (1975) 'A battle won in the war on the paper bureaucracy', *Harvard Business Review*, January–February, pp.8–14.

■ Chapter 13

American Psychiatric Association (1994) *Diagnostic and Statistical Manual of Mental Disorders, 4th edn*, pp.84, 670–71.
D. Burrus (1994) *Techno-Trends: how to use technology to go beyond your competition* (New York: HarperCollins).
R.O. Frost and R.C. Gross (1993) 'The Hoarding of Possessions', *Behaviour Research Theory*, vol. 31, no. 4, pp.367–81.
Andrew M. Seybold (1994) *Using Wireless Communications in Business* (New York: Van Nostrand Reinhold).

■ Other useful publications

There are hundreds of books and articles which provide more information on the topics we have discussed in this book. In addition to the references we have provided for each chapter, we have also compiled a short bibliography of recent publications which we think you may find useful.

□ Getting organised

J. Adair, (1988) *Effective Time Management* (London: Pan Books).
E.C. Bliss (1991) *Getting Things Done* (London: Warner Books).
K. Gleeson (1994) *The Personal Efficiency Program* (New York: John Wiley).
D.L. Lehmkuhl and D.C. Lamping (1993) *Organising for the Creative Person: right-brain styles for conquering clutter, mastering time and reaching your goals* (London: Kogan Page).
S. Winston (1994) *The Organised Executive*, 2nd edn (London: Kogan Page).

□ Computers, technology and information management

M.E. Boone (1993) *Leadership and the Computer* (Rocklin, Cal.: Prima Publishing).
D.A. Wilson (1993) *Managing Information* (Oxford: Butterworth–Heinemann).

□ Self-development and goal-setting

S. Covey and A.R. Merrill (1994) *First Things First* (New York: Simon & Schuster).

∎Index

Accounting Software
  advantages 46
  function 46
Active Storage Area 100, 112, 114
Alesandrini, K. 81
Alice in Wonderland 82
America OnLine 32, 54, 56
American Productivity Center 13
American Psychiatric Association 131, 132
Apple Corp.
  Macintosh 41, 69
  Newton 32, 58, 59, 60
Archive Storage Area 100
Aschner, K. 72
Association of Management 2
Atari 25
Attention Deficit Disorder (ADD) 132

Beard, George x
Being Digital 5, 62
Bell Telephone Company 22
Billing Software
  Advantages 47
  Function 47
Blue Collar Productivity 6
Booher, D 2, 12
Books 32, 72, 74
Borland
  dBase 52
  Paradox 52
  Quattro Pro 45
Brain 108
Brown, A. 12
Burrus, D. 126, 128
Burt, W. A. 66
Business Cards 75
Business Process Re-engineering
  (BPR) 26

Calendars 10, 11
Carroll, L. 82
CD-Rom 5, 23, 32
  advantages 61
  function 61

Champey, J. 26
Clear Desk 99, 106
Clinton, Bill 12
Clippings 103
Clutter 31
Cognitive Psychology 23
Cole, I. 106, 107
Colour 106
Completion 110
CompuServe 32, 54, 56
Computer/Communications
  Convergence 25
Computers
  continuous learning 71
  graphical user interface 41, 118
  learning how to use 69
  learning plan 69
  hardware 9, 33, 58
  laptop 127
  mainframes 58
  mini-computer 58
  mobile 121–6
  networks 9, 32, 33
  notebook 121, 127
  palmtop 127
  peripherals 58
  personal digital assistant (PDA) 58, 121, 127
  software purchase 70
  software upgrades 70
  speech based 39
  sub notebook 121, 127
Conceptual Toolmaking 30
Conceptual Tools 29, 30, 111
Covey, S. 38, 29, 99

Dac-Easy Accounting 47
Dartnell Institute 13
Data Quest Inc. 32
Databases 50, 118
  corporate 19
  pre-formatted 50
  non pre-formatted 52
  flat-file 50
  relational 50

Day-Timer Organiser 54
de Bono, E. 30
Decision-Making School of
    Management 19
DeForest, L. 126
Delphi 32, 54
Denial and Avoidance 90
Diagnostic and Statistical Manual of
    Mental Disorders (DSM-IV) 131
Diaries 10, 32
Digital Documents 63
Digital Video 127
Disney, Colonel 11
Drake, E. L. 125
Drucker, P. 19
Duell, C. H. 126

E-mail 1, 6, 18, 25, 32, 120
    advantages 55
    function 54
Edison, Thomas x
Effectiveness 31
Efficiency 31, 84
Eight Key Information Actions 18–20
Electronic Data Exchange (EDI) 39
Electronic Document Delivery (EDD) 63
Electronic Information 38
    advantages 40
    disadvantages 40
Electronic Organisers 28
Eudora (e-mail system) 56, 120
Executive Information Systems (EIS) 2,
    4, 19
Executive Order No. 937 11

Facsimile 18, 66, 32
Files
    alphabetical order 105
    arrangement 105
    audit 109
    numbering system 105
    filing 3
    filing cabinet 18, 32
Filofax 10, 11
Financial Records 101
Five Technology Potentials 34
Foch, F. 126
Forms 119
Fortune 41
Franklin Ascend 54
Frost, R. O. 131, 132

Getting and Staying Organised 31
Goal-Setting 14

Grocery Shopping 82
Grolier Electronic Publishing 11
Gross, R. C. 131, 132
Guide to Record Retention Requirements
    (US) 102

Hammer, M. 26
Heijn, H. J. 13
Henkoff, R. 41
Hewlett-Packard 125
Hirsch, J. S. 6
Hoover, Herbert 12
Human Computer Interaction (HCI) 66

Industry Week 12
InfoCentral 56
Information
    defined 8, 18
    accessibility (technology potential) 35
    age 125
    breadth (technology potential) 34
    build-up 129
    depth (technology potential) 34
    flow (technology potential) 34, 112
    human perspective 22
    importance 83
    interconnectedness (technology
        potential) 35
    key information actions: change 20;
        communicate 21; create 20;
        discard 21; integrate 20; make
        decisions 21; retrieve 20;
        store 20
    re-engineering 26
    re-engineering benefits 27; improved
        personal effectiveness 27; improved
        team effectiveness 27;
        congruence 27, 28
    re-engineering goals 27; islands of
        information 27; reducing
        information overload 27;
        streamlining 27; accessibility 27
    management systems (MIS) 2
    need for 19
    organisation perspective 22
    overload xi, 2, 14, 25, 125
    personal use of 19
    production 43
    retention strategies 104;
        streamlined 104; super-streamlined
        104; well-stocked 104
    revolution 2, 3
    science 23
    scientist 23

Information *cont.*
  storage   43
  storage concepts   100
  technological perspective   22
  theoretical perspective   22
  theory (communication theory)   22
Infra-red Communications   59
Institute of Management Sciences   22
Intelligent Agents   128
InterDepartmental Statistical Com.   11
Internet   xi, 32, 38, 125
Intuit Quicken   47
Investors Business Daily   32
Invoices   101

Japanese Manufacturing Techniques   23
Jobs, S.   125
Julian and Gregorian Calendar   11
'Just in Time'   (JIT)   23, 113

Kelvin, Lord   125

Leahy, Admiral William   126
Livesay, C.   31
Long-Term Goals   29
Long-Term Planning   29
Lotus
  123   45
  Ami Pro   50
  Approach   52
  Notes   56
  Organiser   51
Lubar, S.   x, xi
Lupton, E.   1

Maedke, W. O.   12
Magazines   72, 73
Mail Merge   49
Malone, T. W.   107
Management
  definition   10
  by walking around (MBWA)   18
  information systems   40
  managing results   14
  science   22
Marks & Spencer   12, 109
Masterthinkers Handbook   30
McGurrin, F. E.   67
MCI Mail   54
Memory   23
  card   58
  chunking   24
  long-term memory   24

prosthesis   113
recognition/recall phenomenon (human memory)   24
short-term memory   23, 113
tip of the tongue phenomenon (human memory)   24
Messy Desk   107
Microsoft Corp
  Access   52
  Bob   51
  Excel   45
  Fox Pro   52
  MS-DOS   41, 68, 118
  Windows   16, 41, 69
  Windows 95   118
  Word   50
Mnemonics   24
Mobile Communications   121–6
  cellular telephones   65; digital   126, 127; analogue   126, 128
  modems   59
  pagers   32, 65
  personal communications network (PCN)   126, 128
Motorola Envoy   60
Multimedia   127
MYOB Accounting   47

National Archives   12
National Association of Professional Organisers   14
National Business Forms Association   12
National Federation of Independent Business   12
Negroponte, N.   5, 62
Newspapers   74
Non-active storage   114
Norman and Hill Ltd   11
Norman, D. A.   68, 113

Obsessive–Compulsive Personality Order   131
Old Farmers' Almanac   5
Operations Research (OR)   22
Ostrom, J. C.   92

PackRat   51
Pack Rat Syndrome   91-94
Panko, R. R.   7
Paper-based Information   9, 33, 38, 72
  administrative requirements   72, 77
  advantages   39
  disadvantages   40

explosion 11
fiscal requirements 72, 78
historical requirements 72, 78
legal requirements 72, 78
operating requirements 72, 73
personal organisers 76
Paperwork Reduction Act (1980) 12
Paranoia 13
Pareto's Principle (80/20 Rule) 29
Peachtree Accounting 47
'Personal', defined 8
Personal Digital Assistant (PDA) 58,
    121, 127
  advantages 59
  function 59
Personal Information Management Strategy
  benefits 84
  benefits quiz 85
  general principles 14–15
  implementing 79–80
  macro approach 95–6
  maintenance 109–15
  micro approach 96
  plan 3
  roadblocks 85
  tools 7
Personal Organiser 72
  advantages 53
  function 53
Personality Disorders 13
Phobias 13
Phonograph x, xi
Place, I. 12
Pophum, E. L. 12
Post-it Notes 32, 72, 75
Presentation Programmes 43
Priority Manager International 54
Problem-Solving Skills 41
Procrastination 87
Prodigy 54, 56
Production Line Model of Work 1
Productivity 6
Professional Organisers 14
Professional Updating 29
Psion Organiser 58, 59, 60
Psychology Today 92
Purchase, A. 7

Quickbooks 47

Rayner, D. G. 12, 109
Re-engineering the Corporation 26

Read Only Memory (ROM) 38
Reagan, Ronald 12
Résumé Programmes 43
Rhodes, J 30
Richard of York Gains Battles in Vain 24
Ridge, W. J. 11
Robbins, A. 38
Robins, A. 28
Roosevelt, Theodore 11
Russell, P. 108

Scanners 39
  advantages 63
  flat-bed 63
  function 62
  handheld 63
  monochrome 63
Scurr, G. 11
Seybold, A. N. 127
Shannon, C. 22
Sharp Wizard 60
Sieff, Sir Marcus 109
Simon, H. 19
Sinclair, I. 11
Split Second Decisions 111
Spreadsheet 43, 118
  advantages 44
  function 44
Star Trek: The Next Generation 39
Starfish Sidekick 51
Stress 2, 84
Surviving Information Overload 81
Symantec *Act* 51

*Taking Control of Your Office Records: A
    Manager's Guide* 72
Tax Records 101
Techno-Trends 126
Technology
  availability 128
  benefits 16
  cost 16, 128
  learning time 16
  life cycle 128
  risk 128
  value 128
Telecommunications 9, 33, 64
Telephone x, 18, 32
Ten Second Filing Operation 90, 110
Thatcher, M. 80
Things That Make Us Smart 68, 113
Thinking 29, 30, 130

154 *Index*

Time 5
  management   xi, 13, 29, 81
  management matrix   29
  management myths   81
Time Manager International 54
Timeslips 48
To-Do List   10, 72, 75
Total Quality Control (TQC)   23
Tracking and Storage Packages
  advantages   57
  function   56
2001: A Space Odyssey   128
typewriter 1, 66
  QWERTY key layout   59, 67
  touch typing method   67

UNIX 41, 68
Unlimited Power 28
Unread Mail   77
*US Labor Department Bureau of Labor
    Statistics* 7
*Using Wireless Communications in
    Business* 127

Value Added Tax (VAT)   102
VCR 5
Visual Clues   41, 106
Visual Memory   106
Voice   120
  Voice-mail   18, 25, 32, 39, 65,
    114

Walking Workers   59
Wall Calendars   72, 76
Wall Street Journal 6
Warner, H. N.   125
Warren, L. W.   92
Watson, T. J.   126
Western Union   125
White Collar Production Line   112
White Collar Productivity 6
WinFax 121
Word Processing   118
  advantages   49
  function   48
Wordperfect 50, 119
Work in Progress Area   100, 112